MURDER & MAYHEM IN SPOKANE

MURDER & MAYHEM IN SPOKANE

DEBORAH CUYLE

THE
History
PRESS

Published by The History Press
Charleston, SC
www.historypress.com

First published 2022

Manufactured in the United States

ISBN 9781540251800

Library of Congress Control Number: 2021952405

Notice: The information in this book is true and complete to the best of our knowledge. It is offered without guarantee on the part of the author or The History Press. The author and The History Press disclaim all liability in connection with the use of this book.

I dedicate this book to all history lovers and true crime explorers—for there is so much fascinating history out there that has been forgotten or simply barely documented at all. As I pored over thousands of pages of old newspapers, I was confused and boggled by how many hideous crimes were committed, some hardly acknowledged. I also found it sad yet humorous that many judges working in nearby cities and towns gave the criminal two choices: either go to their city jail or go to Spokane! Why it became normal to ship local criminals to Spokane was bizarre and perplexing—especially since most of the lawbreakers eventually found their way back to the town they were just banned from, only to commit more crimes.

I also dedicate this book to the many victims who unfortunately lost their lives at the hands of their ruthless murderers. Sometimes their untimely deaths were over a very trivial matter: a few stolen pennies, a misunderstanding or a drunken disgruntlement. No death should be completely forgotten, ever. I hope that by bringing some of these crimes to the surface and making them known, the victims may find some sort of peace.

CONTENTS

FOREWORD

Having worked with Deborah on past materials, I find her writing intriguing and engaging. Having read her work, I enjoy the subtle nuances of her backstory and the lengths she goes to for research in her endeavors. Her ability to go from historical fact-based books to historical fiction is a natural transition we all will enjoy.

Living in Spokane all of my life, and knowing about the history of eastern Washington, I found *Murder & Mayhem in Spokane* easily relatable and factually significant. Deborah's deep knowledge of local history, evident in her writing, made this book a pleasure to read.

You will immediately feel the characters relatable and endearing to your heart and soul. This is a great read for a lazy day of pampering yourself to relaxation; all you need to do is sit back and enjoy hours of mentally running through the streets of Spokane with her to solve (or at least discover) these cases.

—*Mark Porter, researcher*
Spokane, Washington

ACKNOWLEDGEMENTS

There are many people to thank for this endeavor, and without their help and guidance, this book would not have been possible. My wonderful editor, Laurie Krill, has been such a pleasure to work with, along with all of the other incredible people at Arcadia Publishing and The History Press. Their mission to promote local history is passionate and infectious, and I am blessed to work on my books with them. Their dedication to recording local history and people's stories is remarkable, and without them, many books would never be published.

My appreciation and thanks to every single person who does what they can to preserve history—whether it is volunteering at the local historical society or maintaining old buildings that would otherwise be neglected. In this fast-paced and high-tech world, the past can unfortunately be easily forgotten, and every effort to maintain and record valuable data, photographs, diaries, documents and records is of the utmost importance for future generations. I urge people to take the time to learn more about the fascinating history of Spokane and the people who participated in developing it over the past one hundred–plus years!

INTRODUCTION

T he history of old Spokane, Washington, is so full of murders and reckless crimes that every front page of the local newspapers includes some sort of homicide or wrongdoing lurking between the lines. Stories of hundreds of the messy details of violent offenses and sinister dealings literally take over the town's past. In fact, the judges of nearby towns used to give criminals the choice between going to their local jail or disappearing to Spokane! Of course, the convict always took the train ride to his nearby freedom. The town was platted by James Glover in 1878 with just a half-dozen log cabins, and its population soon shot to over 100,000 by 1910. It attracted a cluster of rich men and was considered the "wealthiest city in America" with over 20 millionaires (and 28 half millionaires) living there. But with all this financial glory came dreadful consequences. Violent and unsolved murders, hasty disputes, vicious scandals and hushed suicides were commonplace for Spokane.

Some murders to note were:

- The killing of Spokane police officer George Conniff, who lost his life over the burglary of butter and milk during the Depression era. The crime went unsolved for over fifty years, until a deathbed confession by a fellow policeman and the reopened cold case by Tony Bamonte.
- The Lizzy Borden–style murder of a Spokane businessman named Sloane, hacked to death by his teenage son over twenty-five dollars, his bloody body carted to a back alley via a wheelbarrow.

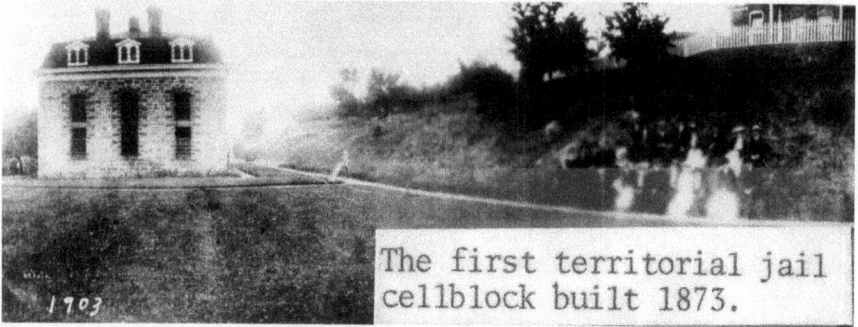

The first territorial jail cellblock built 1873.

Spokane's first territorial jail cell building, in 1903. Some nearby cities would give criminals the crazy option of going to their local jail—or just being sent to Spokane! *Washington State Archives (WSA).*

- The Black Hand gang member who was sent to murder the notorious Frank Bruno, a local Italian saloon owner and sex slave pimp. A crude tattoo scratched into his arm was a silent warning from the gang and became the only clue left behind to help identify the murderer.

These and many more Spokane murders, crimes and unsolved mysteries are to be discovered in *Murder & Mayhem in Spokane!*

PART I
MURDERS

When the fox hears a rabbit scream, he comes running,
but not to help.

—— *Thomas Harris,* Hannibal

Opposite: McNeil Island Federal Penitentiary in 1937. McNeil held inmate Charles Manson from 1961 to 1966 for a federal check forgery charge. *WSA*.

CHAPTER 1
UNSOLVED MURDERS

The Institution as it appeared in 1937.

SPOKANE'S RUTHLESS ITALIAN GANG: THE BLACK HAND

One of the many victims caught in the tangled, brutal web of the Black Hand gang fell prey to foul play in the fall of 1909 in Minnehaha Park near Spokane.

The mangled body of an Italian bodyguard named Ernest Santaro was found stabbed twenty-one times on the grounds of the park. The good-looking Italian man was hired as protection for a local mobster named Frank Bruno. Bruno had a long history of marital, criminal and financial troubles and woes. He was also running a house of prostitution and illegal gambling racket that covered the whole front of a block on Main Street. He was making himself a very wealthy man with his illicit businesses, but his luck would soon run out.

On the fateful night of Santaro's brutal murder, Bruno and Santaro were happily drinking together at Bruno's bar, the Bruno Saloon, located at Front and Browne Streets. They were soon interrupted by a group of angry men who were fighting in front of the bar. Bruno did not want to get involved in any unwanted drama that night, so he gave no attention to the barroom brawl and told Santaro to do the same.

After a few more rounds of drinks, the two men returned to Bruno's house sometime around 7:30 p.m. At the house, they tossed back a final drink and discussed a few loose ends at hand.

They shook hands and said their goodbyes, then Santaro turned and walked down the driveway and into the darkness of the night.

As Bruno quietly closed his front door behind him, he had absolutely no idea this would be the very last time he would see his friend alive.

In the darkness, as Santaro walked back to his own home over in the Hillyard area, he was attacked by unknown assailants. It happened quickly, without warning, and it was brutal.

The next morning, Santaro was found dead with eight stiletto-style knife wounds in his chest, four in his neck and another nine between his shoulders. It was rumored that the stabbings were a vicious payback. Perhaps, in accordance with an old Italian custom, each stab wound represented one of the husbands Santaro wronged by sleeping with their wives; more likely Santaro made someone angry or crossed the wrong person's path.

The killers had cut a crude tattoo into the victim's left forearm. Those who later saw the tattoo quickly crossed themselves for protection—for it was the secret emblem of the Black Hand mob.

The large Black Hand gang spread from coast to coast and was not a mob to be involved with. They would stop at nothing to get their way: arson, bribery, dynamite, blackmail, murder and torture. They had even been known to set fire to children to get their point across. The Black Hand group became so powerful that New York City had to form and utilize its own special task unit to deal with them. They were always on the lookout for two

GIUSEPPE STOLLO.　ANTONIO DE VINCENNO.

Giuseppe Stollo and Antonio De Vincenno, two of the ruthless Black Hand gang leaders the Spokane police were trying to capture. *The* Spokane Press, *December 10, 1906.*

of the Black Hand's most powerful leaders: Giuseppe Stollo and Antonio De Vincenno. So when Black Hand gangsters found their way to Spokane, the local police soon had their hands full.

SPOKANE POLICE BEGAN INVESTIGATING the murder of Santaro and discovered that the evening before his murder, Santaro had tried to get Bruno to stop the fight that was happening between three Italian men in front of his bar. The three men told the officers that Bruno did not want to get involved and decided to ignore the quarrel. Some thought that the arguing men were hired agents of the Black Hand gang who had been hanging out in Spokane lately, spending money lavishly. They were there keeping a watchful eye on Bruno and Santaro, and they'd been ordered to keep tabs on Santaro especially and make sure he did what he was told—*or else they were to kill him*!

The investigators found out that Santaro had shown up only recently from British Columbia with just a few pennies in his pocket, so he borrowed fifty dollars from Bruno to tide him over. Yet somehow, he suddenly managed to have a lot of money that he could squander frivolously. Where *did* all that money come from? Did he not pay (or couldn't pay) back his debts? Did he do a hit for someone? Did he steal it?

THE POLICE WERE TEMPORARILY called from the Santaro investigation and sent to another fiasco: two men were arguing on nearby Front Avenue. Soon a loud *bang, bang* was heard by the patrons on the sidewalk, and the officers rushed to the scene. Black Hand member Rocco Catalano had shot Attalio Mesinaro two times in the hip. The bullets caused so much damage that Mesinaro was not expected to live. When arrested, the men had on them a long stiletto knife and a revolver. They were questioned about Santaro's death. Of course, they claimed they knew nothing.

But after more investigations and interrogations, the events leading up to Santaro's fateful evening began to emerge.

After Bruno and Santaro left the bar to head back to Bruno's home near Minnehaha Park, three mysterious men also took a streetcar toward the park. Back at Bruno's house, Santaro had one more nightcap before leaving the home. The police felt sure that the perpetrators wanted to blackmail Bruno over something and, as a warning, killed his closest friend, Santaro.

The stabbing was brutal. The killers used what is termed a "stiletto" stab. In a stiletto stabbing, the wounds bleed inwardly; the gashes close as

, Mr. O Cassuni. Sir: Tomorrow morning you put $500 in a leather purse, wrap red handkerchief around it and lay it on bench in Mulberry park near northeast corner.. Do this at 7 a. m. and walk away quick. If you turn around you will be shot dead. If you fail we will kidnap your boy, or we will blow up your store with dynamite. We mean business. If you notify the police we will kill you and all your family. Don't fail us, for we are desperate.
                            "BLACK HAND."

A copy of a letter from a Black Hand gang member, using threats and extortion to demand money. *Reprinted in the* Spokane Press, *December 10, 1906.*

the dagger is withdrawn from the body. Yet during the very first stab, there is a large spurt of blood that would mark the killer. Police questioned everyone who lived near Minnehaha Park to see if they saw anyone who had a blood-stained shirt. Again, no one had seen anything.

A poster was printed offering a $500 reward for information leading to the arrest of Santaro's killer.

The officers were certain the murderers were still somewhere in the vicinity of Spokane. After a few more days of questioning locals, they believed the murderer was Joe Barbato (whose new girlfriend was still living with Santaro near Hillyard). Barbato and the woman had recently become lovers, which Santaro did not approve of. Was Barbato's jealousy the motive for the slaying?

Furthermore, it was well known in Spokane that Barbato was inclined to be a violent man. Just the year before, Barbato was working in Frank Bruno's bar on Front and Browne Streets when three men entered the place to enjoy dinner and drinks. After their meal was finished and paid for, the men prepared to leave. Barbato began to get excited and accused the men of *not* paying for their meal. He came out from behind the bar wielding a long, thick ice pick and began attacking the men. His actions led Bruno into a lawsuit for $5,000 brought against him by one of the men, Peter Schwitzer.

The year before that, Barbato was caught slinging his ice pick around again, this time stabbing W. Peters and a woman who was drinking in the bar. He stabbed the woman several times, and the man was injured so badly that he ended up insane! Barbato definitely had anger issues.

At Santaro's funeral, the cops felt there were several secret messages (or codes of some sort) for fellow Black Hand members to recognize, but the police could not decipher them. The coroner revealed that Santaro had been stabbed twenty-one times. Oddly, exactly twenty-one carriages followed Santaro's hearse (four of them were mysteriously empty of any passengers). The police were still baffled by the strange tattoo that had been cut into the dead man's forearm.

The tattoo was of a crude face with a flag underneath it, followed by three lines, a mysterious combination of letters and numbers:

E L S L
1906
A L 7-12

What did the tattoo mean? The police noticed that anyone who saw the tattoo immediately crossed themselves, sensing it was pure evil. Perhaps it was the initials of someone in the gang who had been killed, a gruesome sign of a payback? Did another member get murdered on 7-12-1906? Were their initials A.L.? What did "ELSL" mean? Was it an acronym for something?

The police were baffled, and no one was talking.

AFTER SANTARO'S MURDER, FRANK Bruno (now termed "King of the Dive Keepers in Spokane") and his wife, Philomena, continued to be entangled in all sorts of criminal matters. Philomena eventually began having an affair

Aerial view of the extraordinary Spokane County Courthouse, designed by Willis Richey, who didn't even go to architecture school. He only submitted his drawing because there was a prize for the most original design. *National Archives, War Department, Army Air Forces; June 20, 1941.*

A rare photograph of Frank Bruno, from his passport documents from May 3, 1921. His bodyguard, Ernest Santaro, was found stabbed twenty-one times after he left Bruno's house. *United States Customs.*

with a man named Joe Porttello Princi. Reportedly, she stole $20,000 from Bruno so she and her lover could run away and start a new life together. Bruno promptly filed a complaint, and she was quickly arrested while staying at the Grand Central Hotel in Spokane.

Divorce proceedings began. The angry Frank Bruno ordered a hit on his wife's head for fear she would incriminate him in countless crimes or turn over evidence against him. Mrs. Bruno often told the police she feared for her life.

And she should have been afraid.

In April of 1910, Frank Bruno hired Jim Rolandi, a seventeen-year-old boy, to kill his wife.

Rolandi shot at her on Cook's Hill as she was walking to the courthouse to face her adultery charges. Luckily, she was only shot in the leg.

IN 1910, MORE PROBLEMS came to Spokane. An Italian gang member was shot and killed at 8:25 a.m. on August 23, on the corner of Fourteenth and Wall Streets. Police suspected he was another Black Hand agent sent to Spokane to kill Frank Bruno. The victim was identified as Felica Carrello by a letter found in his blood-soaked pocket. He had been working as a dishwasher at the Davenport Hotel Café for the past two weeks.

When the police arrived, witnesses said they heard three shots fired. Bloody footprints were left next to the victim. Carrello had been shot through his eye and the back of his neck and in the back. Whoever wanted

Felica Carrello was killed on August 23, 1910, on the corner of Wall Street. Police suspected he had been another one of the Black Hand agents sent to Spokane to kill Frank Bruno. Here is Wall Street looking north across Sprague Avenue, with Durkins Liquor on the corner, in 1909. *The E. T. Becher Collection, Spokane Public Library, Northwest Room (SPL/NWR).*

him dead made sure they did the job. Carrello had also suffered from a broken jaw prior to the shootings.

Carrello's body was found by a local teenager named Ben Bullen. His corpse lay behind J.J. Turish's house. Bullen told police that he heard shots fired and then saw a man lying on the ground. He went to investigate. When he discovered the dead man's body, he ran to a neighbor's house in fear.

Detectives Byrnes and Thompson followed the bloody footprints from Carrello's body almost one and a half blocks toward town. They found a revolver about fifty feet from the body. When the detectives ran into nearby patrolman McDonnell, McDonnell told them that he suspected the killer was a man named Frank Albino. Recently, Albino had been drunk in John Nichol's Saloon; he drew his long knife out, began waving it around and threatening patrons, then demanded money from the barkeeper. He was arrested. He had been drunkenly bragging about Santaro's murder.

Another Black Hand agent who had been arrested, Frank Ehrombois, escaped prison when he somehow managed to get free from a chain gang working at the rock pile in Spokane. Did Ehrombois have anything to do with Santaro's murder?

Years later, Spokane's notorious Frank Bruno eventually wound up locked in a cell at McNeil Island Federal Penitentiary on May 17, 1927. He was only thirty-five years old and was sentenced to five years on drug charges. Frank Bruno was no saint. He was born in 1892 and came from Naples, Italy, to New York City on the vessel *Keiserin Maria Teresa* on April 1, 1901. Throughout his life, he was off and on in trouble with the law.

He died in California in 1983.

Note: In 1875, McNeil Island opened as the first federal prison in the Territory of Washington. In 1981, the McNeil Island Federal Penitentiary was renamed the McNeil Island Corrections Center, under the state.

Dynamite Brings Up Bodies

What started as a fun father-and-son fishing trip ended in a double tragedy as their boat hit a large boulder and capsized on May 25, 1909. A.W. Duncan and his son, Ray, age six, were fishing in the river near the foot of Jefferson Street in Spokane. They were swept away by a strong current after their boat flipped. The father tried in vain to save his son from drowning, but in the end, both succumbed to the strong, icy waters.

Rescuers risked their own lives to try to find the victims, but they came up empty handed. After much effort, the plans were abandoned.

Later, more efforts were made using dynamite, in hopes of dislodging the corpses from being trapped underwater.

The process worked; Mr. Duncan's body came to the surface and was found on June 18.

The next day, the body of little Ray was found by Earl and Ray Paterson as they were fishing along the shoreline.

A sad double funeral was planned for the father and son.

But the dynamite originally intended to reveal the bodies of the Duncans brought more than expected. The bloated body of Patrick Corrigan—a Spokane man who went missing on March 20, five days before the Duncans drowned—slowly floated to the surface.

Patrick Corrigan was a trustworthy, middle-aged man with a wife and children, who sold his family farm in Wisconsin and desired to bring his $10,000 to Spokane to invest in land.

Unfortunately, Corrigan may have innocently disclosed his large savings account to the wrong person.

On the morning of the twentieth, he had been spending some time at the house of his sister, Mrs. Miller, at 2605 Sinto Avenue. He told her he was going to go to the grocery store to pick up a few items for dinner and would be back shortly.

That was the last time Mrs. Miller saw her brother alive.

AROUND SEVEN O'CLOCK THAT evening, Corrigan was spotted at P. Heily's Grocery Store at 2613 Sinto Avenue, near the Miller home. When interviewed later, the grocery clerk told investigating detective Fred Pearson that Corrigan seemed confused. Corrigan asked the clerk for directions to his sister's house and asked to be pointed in the right direction. It certainly was odd that he forgot how to get back to his sister's house, just down the same street!

When his body surfaced, it revealed the wounds that he experienced in the agonizing and vicious last few minutes of his life. The coroner determined that Mr. Corrigan had his skull gruesomely crushed and that he had been beaten black and blue. Oddly, most of his clothes were missing from his body, along with his gold watch and chain.

Although no one knew how much cash Corrigan actually had on him at the time of his murder, they found his pockets turned inside out, so the motive was clear. He had almost $7,000 in bank slips in his vest, along with a train ticket recently purchased at the Northern Pacific depot in town for a trip to the opposite coast. His bloated, beaten body was identified by his sad brother-in-law, Henry Miller, a fireman for the Spokane Station No. 8.

Detective Fred Pearson believed that Corrigan had bragged about his recent sale to an opportunistic criminal, who offered to buy him a drink to celebrate the man's good fortune. Pearson believed that Corrigan's drink was laced with an unknown substance that made Corrigan disoriented and confused. He was pretty sure that the murderer followed Corrigan from the grocery store and then took advantage of him being partially inebriated at the time of the attack.

As much as the police tried to find out more about Corrigan's death, the murder remains unsolved to this day and his killer was never found.

A SECOND UNIDENTIFIED BODY also surfaced, but its identity was never confirmed.

DEAD BODY FOUND WHILE FISHING

A young man, age fourteen, named Walter Stack, woke bright and early one day with high expectations for his daily catch. He had been kept up late the night before when he saw a mysterious buggy moving down the lonely Valley Road in front of his house. Stack looked at the clock and noted that it was around midnight. He waited patiently to see if the buggy would return and head back, but it never did.

Sleepy, Stack finally went off to bed.

The next morning, as he gathered his fishing pole and bait, he remembered momentarily the strange buggy he saw the night before. Stack fished all along the river that morning, hoping to find a spot to yield a good catch for dinner. He fished most of the day and then returned home. He noticed nothing out of the ordinary upon his arrival.

THE NEXT DAY, TWO friends, Mat Moore and John Haffton, were killing time by wandering the river looking for cool stones or anything else of interest. Since Moore lived in the Grand Hotel in town and Haffton lived on Fifth Avenue, walks by the water were always a welcome way to enjoy nature and pass the time.

One of the men leaned down to look at something gleaming in the sun, and to his surprise, he found a jackknife! Feeling lucky, they continued their walk down the path along the Spokane River at the foot of the hill…when they stopped dead in their tracks.

Heavy splatters of blood littered the rocks, leaves and dirt on the path. They froze in fear.

Slowly, they continued their walk on high alert.

They soon came across a round iron bar, about one by eighteen inches, that also had blood on it. The men knew that something was not right. As they looked around, they saw what looked like a body about fifty feet away. It was facedown in the bushes and looked as though someone had tossed it over the little hill and let it roll down to the water. There was blood all over the back of the man's skull.

The two men quickly left and went directly to the police station. Detective John McDermott, Sergeant George Hollway and Detective Richard Gemmrig took the case. Moore and Haffton excitedly led the officers back to the spot where they found the body, stuck in the bushes two blocks just below Monroe Street Bridge.

Coroner Smith came along, too, as his services would be needed.

As the group got closer to the victim, they could see that the man had met with foul play. They noted that the body was found approximately at nine o'clock in the morning, July 3,1903. The detectives moved closer and noticed gaseous odors coming from the body. Coroner Smith examined the stranger and told of his findings: the victim had suffered two violent blows to the head, the first one crushing his temple and the second one fracturing his skull at the base of the brain. The man's pockets had been turned inside out and were both empty, suggesting a robbery.

McDermott believed the dead man was the same man he had put under surveillance recently for bootlegging whiskey to the Indians. Unfortunately, the man's face was almost unrecognizable. They did note that he was clean-shaven, about thirty years old and wearing blue overalls.

Gemmrig firmly believed the man was murdered elsewhere and dragged to the spot where he was dumped in Peaceful Valley. He noted that, since there were only small splotches of blood and not large bloody areas, this indicated he was pretty much dead when they dumped him.

Coroner Smith felt confident that the man was murdered by the Indians for some sort of revenge. He thought, due to the gaseous nature of the body, that the victim had been dead for two or three days.

When they questioned the Stack boy, he told them that he had not seen the dead man, the coat, the handkerchief or the iron bar when he had walked the same shoreline earlier.

The killer or killers were never apprehended, and the victim was never positively identified.

The case remains cold and unsolved to this day.

CHAPTER 2

FORGOTTEN MURDERS

*"Why does anyone commit murder?" he asked in a low voice. "I—" I blinked.
"How should I know?" "Three reasons," Christopher said. He held up one
finger. "Love." Another finger. "Revenge." And finally, a third finger. "Profit..."*
—Meg Cabot

Body Shot and Burned at Fort George Wright

The horrific murder of a Polish immigrant named John Saudawski (also known as Jan Lewandoski) in March 1909 shocked the residents of Spokane. His partially burned body was found on a knoll on the Fort George Wright military reservation. His charred remains were a gruesome and disturbing discovery.

The last time Saudawski was seen alive, he was with a coworker, a German immigrant named Paul Clein (1873–1914), also known as Paul Krasnensky, Krasienusky and Wilson. They both worked for Bernard Weisman at his cabinet shop in the city. Since the two both worked as cabinetmakers and both were immigrants, they struck up a friendship.

On March 1, Clein and Saudawski were seen together eating at a German bakery in Spokane. The men were discussing taking jobs in British Columbia that would pay them better: seven dollars per day.

Three weeks later, on March 21, Sergeant Lathoff stumbled upon a gruesome sight. Not only had Saudawski suffered from being burned, but

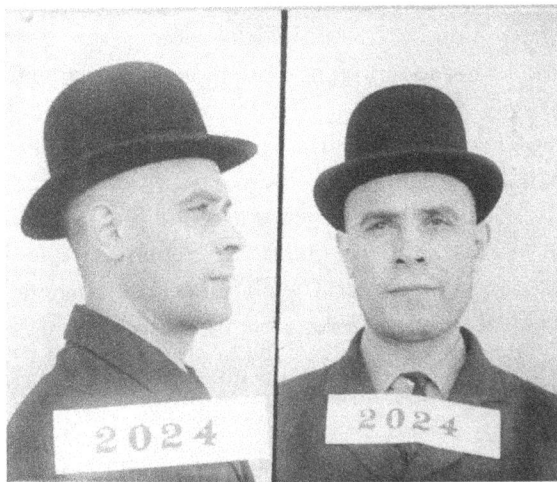

Killer Paul Clein murdered John Saudawski in 1909. Saudawski's partially burned body was found on a knoll on the Fort George Wright military reservation. *United States Penitentiary McNeil Island, Washington, Photos and Records of Prisoners (USP/MNI).*

he also had two bullets from a .32-caliber revolver in his body: one in his neck and one in his skull.

Since Clein was the last one seen with the dead man, he immediately became the prime suspect.

CLEIN CLAIMED HE WAS previously a member of the mounted police in British Columbia and had served in the German army. He boasted that he could speak several languages. These facts did not impress the Spokane officers, and they continued to question him for several days. Eventually, Clein admitted to eating dinner with Saudawski but claimed that he was innocent of killing him.

But Clein's credibility quickly crumbled. The officers discovered that Clein had recently pawned a gun—the same caliber gun that had killed the victim. Clein denied ever pawning a gun and told investigators that he had given his gun to his fiancée, Mrs. Ida Douglas, and that *she* must have sold it.

When questioned, Ida did not deny or confirm these facts.

Investigators learned that Clein had been staying at the Lynne Hotel and sharing a room with Joe Schultz. The police quickly made their way to his room to search for evidence. In Clein's trunk, they found documents that proved his real name was Paul Krasnensky. This was not too alarming, as people in that era often changed their names. They also found that he had an ex-wife and twins in Canada, but only one of the children was still alive and was living in a foster home. They found a stack of love letters from a high-priced beautiful blonde prostitute named May (Mae) Randall, who lived in Kalso, British Columbia. In one of the letters, May was responding to Clein's request for her to send him more money. He claimed he was dead broke.

People told the police that Clein had been griping about his finances for several days before Saudawski's murder. When interrogated, he did have thirty dollars in cash in his vest, and when the police asked him about this money, he told them that he "always has thirty dollars on his person."

The most incriminating evidence against Clein's innocence was the discovery of Saudawski's personal cabinetmaking tools and his phonograph in Clein's room. *Why would he have Saudawski's tools and talking machine?*

"I took them on a thirty-five-dollar debt he owed me before he left town," was Clein's answer.

They handcuffed him and carted him off to the police station, where he would be charged with Saudawski's murder.

BACK AT TURNBILL AND Company's Undertaking, coroner Schlegal performed an autopsy on the victim. Saudawski had some beans that were undigested in his stomach, which led Schlegal to conclude that he had been murdered between two and four hours after he dined with Clein. He had bullets in both his neck and head. Schlegal also determined that the victim had been dead and exposed to the elements for around three weeks.

BACK AT THE STATION, Clein continued to profess his innocence to anyone who would listen. Then he begged the police to let him go, so *he* could catch the killer himself. He told the *Spokane Press*, "I will secure his conviction with stronger testimony than circumstantial evidence. What can a man do cooped up in here?"

The entire precinct laughed out loud at his proposal.

Clein claimed that the *real* killer was a man who roomed with him named Paul Fuchs.

The police continued with their investigation against Clein.

Clein's credibility continued to worsen. The police discovered that he was engaged to *two* women at the same time. And the two women did not know about each other...until now. The smooth-talking liar had been caught by more than the police!

As the trial moved on, witnesses began to come forward to the police with their information.

An elderly woman named Mrs. Ella Newkirk was perhaps the most damning to Clein's case. She lived in a house just north of the Fort George Wright reservation. The night of March 1, she was startled by the sound of a gunshot in the direction of the fort. The shot was followed by two awful and gruesome screams. Then she heard a couple more shots being fired. She did not sleep well that night.

The following morning, Tuesday the second, as Ella cautiously peered out her window, she noticed a black horse hitched to a distinctive, rubber-tired buggy passing by. She tried to impress in her memory the face of the driver—*just in case.*

Later, she immediately recognized Clein's face during the trial.

Joe Schultz, the roommate of Clein's, also destroyed Clein's story. Clein told police that he left Saudawski with an unknown man who wanted to buy the phonograph. A few days later, the same man sold Clein the machine. Schultz denied the whole story and said there was never a man involved in buying the phonograph.

A young boy named Glen Smith who worked for the Keystone Stables in Spokane told the court that he had rented a black rig with rubber tires to Clein on March 2 from 6:30 to 8:30 a.m. When the man returned the buggy, he told the boy that he had "lost all his money playing poker" and he "needed to go to his home at Fort Wright to get some." This was the same

A boy, Glen Smith, worked for the Keystone Stables (much like the one shown) in Spokane and rented a black rig with rubber tires to Paul Clein on March 2, 1909. *SPL/NWR.*

exact buggy that Ella saw Clein driving past her house that morning. The buggy was not easy to miss; it had bright yellow running gears. Others saw the buggy in the vicinity of Fort George Wright military reservation that morning as well. The wheel tracks leading to the area where the body was found matched those of the buggy Clein rented perfectly.

B.R. Hunt, an express man who was working late on March 1, told the police that Clein approached him on the street around midnight and demanded he haul a long, wooden box about six feet in length from Spokane to Garden Springs. He simply told Clein, "I will not work at night!" Now he was sure the box had contained the corpse of Mr. Saudawski.

Bernard Weisman, Clein and Saudawski's employer, stated that Clein had come into work two hours late that morning. He denied that Clein ever called him to let him know he was going to be late, as Clein had told the jury.

A man named Charles Anderson, who ran the Miner's Hotel, blew Clein's story about the gun out of the water, as he told the court that he had witnessed an argument between Clein and another patron, during which Anderson had to take a .32-caliber pistol from Clein. Clein had stated he had no such gun. This was the same type of gun that killed Saudawski.

The jealous lover, May Randall (a housekeeper who claimed she was also Clein's fiancée and insisted Clein was innocent early on in the investigation), now dropped a large sack of love letters on the desk of the prosecutor for good measure. Clein's other lover, Ida Douglass, was crying alligator tears on the witness stand but soon refused to perjure herself for him. Manipulating two innocent and loving women at the same time did not go over well with the jury.

CHARGES WERE BROUGHT UP against Clein. His motive was robbery (although he somehow missed the forty dollars that was still tucked inside Saudawski's vest pocket). He was convicted of murder in the Spokane courtroom and sentenced to death.

On January 4, 1910, Clein was granted a new trial based on the determination of whether Saudawski's murder took place on state or federal land. His new attorney argued that since Saudawski's body was found on federal land, the case would have to be tried by a federal court. Matters dragged on and on until May 22, 1911. Finally, the whole ordeal came to a halt for the attorneys and worn-out judges. Clein was found guilty of murder a second time and sentenced to life in prison. He was moved to the McNeil Island Federal Penitentiary. He lived his miserable existence in his cell until May 20, 1914, when he died under unknown circumstances.

KILLED OVER BAD HANDWRITING

Officer Herndon tried to appear calm as he arrived at the bloody scene in Ti Gee's joint on First Avenue, opposite the No. 1 fire station in Spokane.

The victim was Lee Tung, a local Chinese man. The killer? Gin Pong, his roommate. Both men had been recently released from jail.

The Chinese underground world in Spokane during the late 1890s circled around illegal gambling, excessive opium smoking and the sex slavery of Chinese (and French) women. The group of Chinese had their own form of punishment and settled any disagreements among themselves. An eye for an eye, they believed.

This particular night, Tung was busy writing out New Year's cards. As Pong walked by, he noticed Tung working on the stack of cards and stated to Tung that he did not like the man's handwriting. Irritated, Tung shot back, "I wish bad luck on you for one year!"

Pong became furious at Tung's wicked spell.

He went into his room, came back with a large club and began beating the man. Tung had a knife on him, but it did not offer much protection from the larger Pong. When Pong decided the club wasn't enough, he went and grabbed two hatchets—one for each hand—and began hacking Tung to pieces. When *that* still wasn't enough to quiet his anger, he decided to stab Tung in the heart a few times for good measure with a butcher knife.

After his fury ran its course, Pong realized what he had done.

He wanted to cover up his grisly attack with the false pretense of self-defense, so Pong slit his own throat with the bloody knife.

The Chinamen nearby decided this crime might be better for the local authorities and quickly summoned the Spokane police.

When Officer Herndon questioned witnesses to the gory job, they soon revealed the truth. Tung didn't stand a chance against the violent and larger Pong. One witness told Herndon, "The other Chinamen all say that Gin Pong is a bad man, and he ought to have been killed a long time ago!"

Pong was promptly arrested and thrown into jail, howling with his strange and creepy laughter the whole time.

He was convicted of murder in the first degree and sentenced to hang on August 20, 1896. For some reason, his execution was delayed and rescheduled for April 30, 1897. When the time came, Sheriff Christopher C. Dempsey had a huge scaffold erected in the jail yard across from the courthouse for the event. He even made sure that Pong could watch the gallows being built from the window in his cell. Invitations were sent out to a select hundred people to come watch the hanging of Pong. His punishment excited so much interest that Dempsey soon had to order a gigantic circus tent to be assembled over the scaffolding to prevent the crowd from watching the man swing.

But it did not stop the over-curious locals from their fascination with Pong. Over four thousand spectators crowded the jail in order to peer in and get a good glimpse of Pong before he died.

Pong was not bothered by this attention.

The morning of his execution, he remained calm. He rose as usual, exercised, bathed and put on his new suit. He even requested a new pair of shoes and a shave for the event. His imminent execution did nothing to diminish his hearty appetite. He consumed three pork chops, three fried eggs, eight slices of toast, three baked potatoes and two cups of coffee.

A couple hours later, Pong was hungry again and demanded a second meal. Surprisingly, he was granted his wish and ravenously ate fried chicken with French fries and tea and more toast.

At precisely 12:03 p.m. on April 30, the lever was pulled, and Pong swung to his death.

Seventeen minutes later, he was pronounced dead.

All of that drama because he did not like his roommate's handwriting!

SHERIFF GEORGE CONNIFF: KILLED OVER MILK AND BUTTER

The Depression brought about great misery in the United States, and many families went without any substantial food. Dairy items like milk and butter became ridiculously expensive, a luxury only the rich could afford. Soon, bootlegging of dairy products and a wide range of robberies began. Creameries had to have security officers to protect their valuable wares. Runners would steal the items in great demand and transport them across the borders to sell on the black market. Hard-to-get items such as cigarettes and cigars were also a hot target, so tobacco warehouses were constantly being robbed. These stolen items were then smuggled into and sold through a place called Mother's Kitchen in Spokane, a local police hangout. Mother's Kitchen was owned and operated by Virgil Burch (later suspected of George Conniff's murder). When Detective Sonnebend tried to investigate the staff, he was blocked by his superior, Sergeant Daniel Mangan.

In the fall of 1935, a call came in concerning a robbery in progress at the Newport Creamery. Sheriff George Edwin Conniff Sr. (1882–1935) immediately went to the area, prepared to make an arrest.

At around 10:00 p.m., he caught three men prowling in the alley behind the creamery in the act of robbing the business, and soon shots were fired.

Never in his wildest nightmares did Conniff expect to be dead ten hours later, shot over such items as butter and milk!

Conniff was shot multiple times. The thugs got away without leaving a single clue. Conniff was rushed to a hospital in Spokane, but they were unable to save the officer. He was only fifty-three years old.

Sheriff Elmer Black, Conniff's close friend, was determined to find his partner's killers. Yet after months of trying to close the investigation, he came up empty handed.

The case went cold and, sadly, Conniff's murder remained unsolved.

Twenty years later, in 1955, Spokane detective Charles Sonnebend reported that he knew who had killed Conniff. He gave the information to a Seattle prosecutor. He also said that in 1935 he had arrested Acie Logan for auto theft and several other crimes. Sonnebend said that when he questioned Logan about the murder, Logan told him that Clyde Willis Ralstin (1899–1990, a former Spokane police detective) and another cop were the ones who killed Conniff.

With this new information, Sheriff Black reopened the unsolved murder case. But tragically, just a few months after Black reopened the case, he suspiciously "fell" from an interstate bridge.

Unfortunately, the Conniff case again went to the bottom of the pile, still unsolved.

That is, until 1985, when another Spokane sheriff named Tony Bamonte (1942–2019) took charge and reopened the cold case once again. Determined to get to the bottom of Conniff's murder, Bamonte began interviewing former detectives, relatives and criminals. One witness, Pearl Keogh, came forward with some valuable information. She told Bamonte that Virgil Burch was involved, along with Clyde Ralstin and Acie Logan. She revealed that, in 1940, Burch confessed to the tragic killing to her husband. Burch also made another chilling claim: Detective Ralstin intentionally covered

The gun that killed Sheriff George Conniff in 1935 was found by Sheriff Tony Bamonte in 1985 under the Post Street Bridge. This photograph shows the bridge in 1936, one year after Conniff's murder. *SPL/NWR.*

up the crime! (Ralstin checked out a .32 revolver just a few days prior to the killing and later reported the gun "stolen.")

Four years later, more witnesses began to emerge. Two of significance were Daniel Mangan and Bill Parsons, both Spokane police officers at the time of Conniff's death. They stated that, back in 1935, they were ordered by their superior (name not mentioned) to "dispose of a package" in the Spokane River.

The package felt like a gun.

Parsons and Mangan drove to the Post Street Bridge and threw it over the side and into the deep river below.

The gun remained hidden under the Spokane River's icy waters for over fifty years...

BAMONTE CONTINUED TO SEARCH for clues; he desperately wanted to solve the case, and he was sure he could find the gun somehow. He got his break in 1989 when the Washington Water and Power Department dammed the river for inspection and maintenance purposes. A once-in-a-lifetime opportunity: the Spokane River would be dry exactly where Bamonte reckoned the gun would still be! Quickly, Bamonte grabbed his metal detector and headed for the riverbed below the bridge.

And right where Bamonte figured the hidden gun might be, there it was, nestled in between a few rocks—with fifty years of corrosion on it.

(Note: The weapon can currently be seen in a display case in the Joel E. Ferris research room at the Northwest Museum of Arts & Culture, located at 2316 West First Avenue in Spokane.)

Acie Logan ended up jailed at McNeil Federal Penitentiary and became inmate #11819, booked on interstate theft charges on November 15, 1935. A longtime criminal, he was previously booked at Idaho State Penitentiary on robbery and interstate theft charges.

Former Spokane detective Clyde Ralstin was fired from the Spokane Police Department. He left Spokane in 1937, two years after the murder. Although many claimed he was directly involved, and may have been the killer, Ralstin continued to insist he was innocent and remained a free man. He took his final breath in Montana on January 23, 1990, and some say he confessed to the murder of Conniff right before he died.

Worden Spinks (also known as Edward Davies) was also implicated as one of the young men who was robbing the creamery the night of Conniff's murder. He had a long history of theft and assault. He spent time in the Idaho State Penitentiary as inmate #3768.

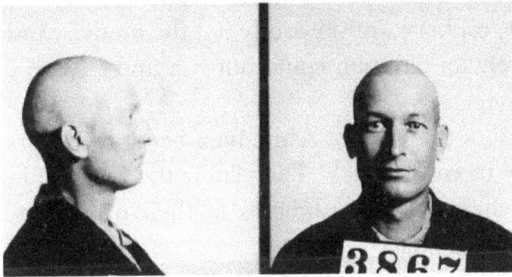

Top: Acie Logan was arrested for involvement in the 1935 robbery of the Newport Creamery and the murder of Sheriff George Edwin Conniff Sr. *USP/MNI.*

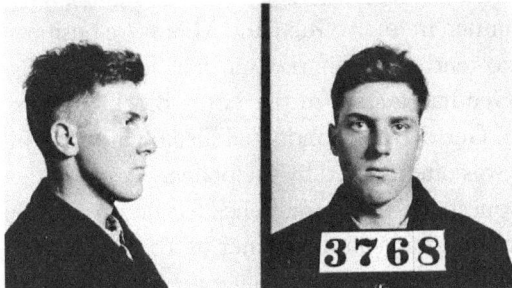

Bottom: Worden Spinks was arrested as one of the men who was robbing the creamery the night of Conniff's murder. *WSA.*

Thanks to the excellent patience, detective skills and determination of Sheriff Tony Bamonte, the fifty-year-old murder has been solved. Rest in peace, George Conniff Sr. and Tony Bamonte.

The Chinamen Murders

Four Chinamen were busy working in Spokane at their street market in June 1907, as they did every other day, but this day would soon come to a tragic and bloody end. Before midnight, two of the four men would end up dead and on slabs at Smith Undertaking Company, a third lying on the brink of death at Sacred Heart Hospital.

Mr. How Guen was shot straight through his heart by the attacker and died instantly. Sen Men was shot two times in his abdomen and was rushed to Sacred Heart, where he soon died. Ah So took a bullet through his right lung and was also rushed to Sacred Heart. The fourth man was an elderly gentleman named Sho Lap, who was found hiding underneath a bed, frightened half to death.

Sheriff Doak and Deputy Mac Pugh rushed to the scene of the crime. They interviewed every person within one hundred yards, but no one was talking. "White man, cloth on face," was all the Chinamen would repeat. The weapon used, they determined, was a .38-caliber revolver. Doak and Pugh noticed that all three men were shot from the front. Since the victims still had money in their pockets, robbery was obviously not the motive. And why was Sho Lap spared? Surely an old man could not run and get away from such aggressive killers.

Wary, the officers suspected that the story of white men being the killers was concocted to simply throw them off track. They knew the Chinese in Spokane wished to mete out their own punishments in their own ways, without the involvement of the local police.

The officers quickly discovered that there had long been an ongoing feud between several groups of Chinamen in town. Guen and Men were business partners, and they were hired to tend to the market gardens for a wealthy Chinese man named Ti Gee. Gee had a store in the Lotus Block building near the Spokane police station. Gee actively conducted illegal gambling in the back of his building, which was often raided by the police.

A man named Ah Yeck was questioned, and the police felt he was acting very suspiciously. Yeck ran an opium joint on the corner of Fourth Avenue and Browne Street. Rumor was that Yeck had tried to get the Holt brothers from Garden Springs to kill two of Gee's men. They refused. There was much rivalry and anger between Ah Yeck and the murdered men. The police also discovered that there *were* two white men on the scene the night of the shooting.

Regardless, Ah Yeck was handcuffed and taken to the county jail by Detectives Doak and Pugh on suspicion of killing the two men and injuring Ah So.

Yeck was very high on opium at the time of his arrest. An addict, after spending a day or so in jail, Yeck began having withdrawals from the dope. The officers convinced him that if he came clean, he could have his opium pipe back. Shaky and irritated, Yeck still had nothing to say. Finally, the police were able to secure over a dozen witnesses to Yeck's whereabouts during the shooting, so he was released and free to go and get high.

Another man, a white man named Lee Reiger, was arrested on suspicion, but he was also later released.

Ti Gee left Spokane in the year 1909 to return to his homeland, China.

The case went cold, and no one was ever convicted of the murders. To this day, the brutal murders of How Guen and Sen Men remain unsolved.

JEALOUS HUSBAND SHOOTS HIS BUSINESS PARTNER

One Monday night in October 1904, the sound of bullets rang through the streets of Spokane.

Otis Claud, his wife and his business partner, H.C. Stiles (who worked as the cook), were closing up the place after a long day. Soon, their lives would be changed forever.

MR. CLAUD WAS KNOWN to be a very jealous man, and his wife was tiring of his antics. She had reported to the police multiple times that he often chased her and threatened to kill her. Finally, she had had enough; she was going to leave him.

But Claud would not stand for it. Blind with anger, he decided he would put an end to all of it. After closing the Broadway Café on the night of the tenth, Mrs. Claud left the restaurant and headed for home. Stiles finished cleaning up the kitchen, then left to go into town. Claud decided to follow him. After a few twists and turns, Stiles realized that Claud was hot on his heels, and he couldn't shake him.

Mrs. Claud had actually gone to the police department, not her home, to report her husband's threats of killing her once again. She also wanted to collect from Stiles the twenty-five dollars in receipt money for the day, so she could have money to run away from her jealous husband and Spokane forever.

STILES, TRYING TO ELUDE Claud, had ducked into the Theater Comique, hoping to rid himself of the pesky husband. But soon the door to the theater opened and Claud came barging in, his face red with rage.

Mrs. Claud, done at the police department, was soon stopped out front of the theater (where she was supposed to meet Stiles) in her carriage. The men took their fight out into the street. The hot-tempered Claud pulled out his revolver and began shooting at everyone. He aimed at his stunned wife and fired two shots directly at her; she quickly fell from the carriage. Claud shot a few more times, this time hitting Mr. Stiles twice: one bullet in his right shoulder and another in his hip.

Officer Roff, who was nearby, rushed to the scene. Patrolman William Dial (who was on Howard Street near Riverside) also heard the commotion and ran to the scene. Roff had seen Claud fire his gun, so he fired a warning shot over the man's head, but Claud completely ignored it. A waiter named Robert Hoffman tried to help the officers, grabbing Claud from behind. Just then, Claud turned his attention to Dial, pointed his gun at the officer and pulled the trigger. Alarmed, Dial fired two times back at Claud. One bullet struck waiter Hoffman's hand and blew his finger clear off! Claud continued to shoot at Dial, but luckily, Claud's gun was now empty.

Officer Dial's second bullet had pierced Claud in his stomach, and he fell to the ground. The officers quickly apprehended him. Mr. Stiles rushed to Mrs. Claud and helped her to her feet. "Are you shot?" he asked. "Yes," she said weakly, "twice."

Strangely, as the police were dragging Claud off, Mr. Stiles decided to try to walk to his apartment at 1321 Broadway Avenue. There his shocked roommate, Ralph Sheppard, tried to assist Stiles with his bullet wounds. The injuries were substantial, though, and Stiles also went to Sacred Heart.

Mr. Otis Claud died within a few hours of being shot.

Mrs. Claud was attended to by the doctors, and it was determined she would survive the assault. Weak and terrified, she told the coroner that her husband had been crazy with jealousy.

Officer Dial was pardoned from any blame in the killing of Claud because Claud continued to shoot at Dial, even though he apparently had run out of bullets.

A man named George P. Cooper soon took over the café at 1009 Broadway Avenue.

No more is known about whether or not Mrs. Claud and Mr. Stiles continued the affair that led to her husband's death.

BETTER OBEY THE CARONS

The first decade of Spokane was one riddled with violence, prostitution and lawlessness.

One French couple who moved to town, Leon Caron (Tireux) and Lucy Caron, were despicable, to say the least. They brought over dozens of innocent young girls at a time, tricked them into thinking they would be working in an office and then forced them into prostitution. Spokane had its own sex slave ring, and Leon Caron was the Big Boss. You did not cross the Carons, because if you did, you would end up dead. They used people like property, with no regard for their safety or health. The police were constantly arresting the Carons for "importing women for immoral purposes." In 1902, Sheriff Martin Burns was busy again arresting the Carons for bringing girls into the United States illegally. In 1903 and 1904, the Carons again pled guilty to the same charges.

Local citizens felt the Carons were the vilest parasites of Spokane. They kept their lodging houses in an area called the Old Dive Division.

One of Caron's slaves was named Theresa Martini. She did not want to comply with the Caron rules, and she became very defiant. That was the last anyone saw of poor Theresa Martini.

One day an old man named Olaf Johnson couldn't find his cat. He thought it might be hiding under his porch at 14 South Jefferson Street in Spokane.

What he found was more than his cat. The grisly remains of a female skeleton

Thomas Maloney was McNeil prison's warden from 1919 to 1921. By 1931, the prison had acquired 2,107 acres. *WSA.*

41

were partially buried under his porch! Oddly, the bones had a knife buried with them.

The Carons were immediately suspected and arrested again, but this time they were not going to be released. They pled guilty once again, and this time they were both sent to McNeil Island Federal Penitentiary. They were to be held for a minimum of three years.

Leon Caron (Tireux) was transferred from McNeil Island prison to a hospital in Tacoma, Washington, on November 22, 1904. There is no more information about him except that he died before he finished serving his sentence.

Lucy Caron had been sent to McNeil Island in 1903 and was scheduled to be released for good behavior on May 29, 1905.

CATTLE RUSTLING DON'T PAY

The Pershall gang would soon find out that stealing cattle didn't always pay.

The gang had been terrorizing local ranchers far and wide for years, but it all came to a violent end when Deputy Sheriff James Logan and George Sweet went on a manhunt for the gang in the summer of 1909.

It was a shootout that made the news for weeks, resulting in the death of a gang member named Bascom Wallace, age thirty. The shootout occurred near Nine Mile Bridge in Spokane. Officer Sweet told the *Spokane Press* on June 15, "I said, 'Hands up, boys!' and bullets flew. At least sixteen shots were fired. I emptied the six chambers of my revolver before the smoke of the battle cleared. I had two guns with me and emptied both of them."

Wallace was shot in the back and instantly killed. His partner, Tom Greenman, was shot but was able to get away on horseback, leaving a trail of blood. The nearby cattle were frightened and began running toward the other mounted officers, Chief Deputy Clarence Long and Deputy Sheriff S.D. Doak.

It was no mystery that the Pershall brothers had been cattle rustling for many years and selling the stolen stock to a man in Spokane. Later, a rancher named Bryan stopped by Pugh's office to drop off a current warrant for Wallace's arrest for thirty cattle that Wallace had stolen from him earlier.

A wanted poster was printed for the body of Tom Greenman, wanted dead or alive.

Once Greenman found out he had a wanted poster out for him and a bounty on his head, he turned himself in at the sheriff's office.

Another gang leader, Dwight Pershall, was also found guilty, along with Ewing Pershall. The judge found Wallace's murder justifiable. The rustlers were all sentenced to one to ten years at the Walla Walla State Penitentiary.

A Frozen Baby and a Jealous Husband

Another prisoner who was incarcerated in McNeil Island Federal Penitentiary multiple times was a ruthless, abusive and manipulative man named Raleigh M. Faulkner. His ability to con his lovers, the public, judges and police officers was nothing less than bizarre. Even with his long list of criminal charges, he continued to get released from (or sometimes even avoid) prison.

Faulkner married a young girl named Blanche when she was just sixteen years old. Only a few months into their marriage, he began to abuse her and threaten to kill her if she ever left him. But after years of abuse and the birth of their daughter, Bessie, Blanche decided she wanted a better life for herself and her baby. Her parents snuck her out of the Faulkner house at midnight, and she was whisked off to Seattle, Washington, to live her life without fear and raise her baby in a safe environment. She quickly filed for a divorce.

But Faulkner had other plans. He followed her to Washington.

Bessie filed charges against her soon-to-be ex, and he was thrown into a Seattle jail for threatening to kill his wife—and only received a three-month sentence. He was released because he told the judge that he would "behave." Lying through his teeth, he convinced the courtroom that he wanted to reform himself this time and do the right thing. "I have no more interest in my wife and will not molest her. I will speak with her and nothing more. I will not molest her, although she has betrayed me."

Instead, he discovered the locale where his wife and their baby were hiding from him. He marched right up onto the porch at 1523 Seventeenth Avenue South and loudly banged on the door. (He did not know that his wife was actually living in a tiny cabin *behind* the Harbin home.) Mrs. Harbin, dressed in her curlers and nightclothes, hesitantly answered the door. After a few words, the woman soon recognized the stranger as her boarder's abusive husband. She tried to slam the door on him; he attempted to force his way into the home. Just then, Mr. Harbin appeared, confused, also dressed in nightclothes. Suddenly awake, he immediately tried to protect his wife from the stranger. He pushed Faulkner back out onto the porch. After a brief struggle, Faulkner frantically stabbed the man in his back. Even though Mr. Harbin was now bleeding profusely, the two continued to fight out into the front yard. William Lewis, Harbin's half-brother, heard the men struggling and quickly came to assist Harbin against his attacker.

Then Harbin was stabbed a second time, near his heart. Weakened, he barely made it to the front gate before he fell, fighting for breath. Lewis and Faulkner continued to rumble, and the latter fell and went tumbling down the hill, where he lay stunned for a moment or two. Lewis ran back over to Harbin. While Lewis and Mrs. Harbin were tending to Mr. Harbin's wounds, Faulkner was able to make his getaway.

It had only been eight hours since he convinced the judge to release him and drop the case against him because he promised to be on his best behavior!

The judge really should have known better than to trust this criminal.

Just a few months earlier, Faulkner had kidnapped his three-year-old daughter and made his way back to Spokane. (Prior to that, he threatened to kill his mother-in-law if she didn't hand over the child.) A telegram was immediately sent out to the patrolmen in Spokane from Seattle. Only seventeen minutes later, they found Faulkner walking on Sprague Street, and he was promptly arrested and put into jail.

When the police questioned him about the whereabouts of Bessie, Faulkner told them that his wife had cheated on him, that *she* had stolen the baby from him and that now he had hidden the child in an unheated shack out in the woods. The police panicked, for it was winter and snow covered the ground. No matter how much they questioned Faulkner, he refused to tell them where he had hidden Bessie. If the poor child wasn't found soon, she would surely die. It had already been three days, Faulkner warned the authorities. Better be quick!

Spokane's captain of police, G.G. Miles, ordered Detectives Hogan and Thompson to search everywhere for the poor child. They were not to leave a single stone unturned.

The angry captain told Faulkner, "If that child dies, you will be charged with murder!"

Faulkner seemed unintimidated. He calmly told Miles, "If the child dies, it would be dead, that's all there is to it. It will have to stay dead. I am not going to let my wife have the baby again!" Then, strangely, he begged to be released so he could go fetch the child himself.

He was refused. He had already been arrested several times for abusing his wife. He was a pure scumbag to also now be threatening the life of his child!

Raleigh M. Faulkner had a strange ability to con his lovers, the public, judges and police officers. Even with his long list of criminal charges, he continued to get released from (or sometimes even avoid) prison. *USP/MNI.*

Poor Blanche had to read about her child's welfare in the papers. She became frantic with worry and almost hysterical. The police could still not find Bessie, even though they searched every square inch of the snow-covered forest near Spokane.

A tip finally came in, giving the police a break. The child was actually being cared for at the Windsor Hotel in Spokane; little Bessie was safe and sound.

FAULKNER CONTINUED TO BE in and out of prison for all sorts of charges: forgery, assault, counterfeiting, fraudulent banknotes and smuggling whiskey from a Northern Pacific Railroad yard in Seattle.

He was known mostly as prisoner #2185 while in McNeil Island Federal Penitentiary.

SCHULTZ: KILLED OVER A PAYCHECK

A hardworking and well-liked forty-five-year-old man named Perry Schultz came to Spokane looking for work in 1907 and landed a job as a motorman for the Traction Company. He had been working for the company for six months and saving up his money. He was hoping to get a job with the Great Northern Railroad as a switchman.

But late on December 8, 1907, as Schultz was sleeping after a hard day's work, his slumber was interrupted by the sounds of a robber. A struggle ensued between Schultz and the unknown assailant, and a gunshot was heard reverberating in his room.

Schultz was left for dead and bleeding on the floor in his room at the Kaiser Hotel in Spokane.

IN THE NEXT ROOM over, a man named Curtis Hawkenberry was disturbed by noises of a struggle. He later told police, "I went to my room about 2:00 a.m. and was writing. I had just gone to bed when I heard the sound of a struggle and then a report [shot]. I dressed and quickly notified Charles Sigler, the night clerk at the hotel, that a man had been murdered."

The night clerk quickly summoned the police. After the shots rang out, Curtis Hawkenberry and Joe Gregg, bartenders at the hotel, were the first people at the scene.

Chief of Police Rice was soon at the scene. He questioned everyone about the murder. Coroner Witter also came to the hotel. He discovered that Schultz's door was wide open. The victim had a bullet from a .32-caliber pistol in his left arm and another in his chest. He had been badly bruised, and signs of blunt force trauma about the head and body were evident. Rice believed that Schultz had fallen victim to a robbery, yet he was suspicious of both Gregg and Hawkenberry. When Hawkenberry and Gregg's rooms were searched, Rice found several incriminating items.

A set of skeleton keys and a key nipper were found, both items used by burglars. There was also a .38-caliber cartridge found on the floor in Hawkenberry's room, but he denied knowing why it was there.

When the police spoke to the night clerk, he had an interesting twist: "Hawkenberry came down the stairs and said, 'A man has been murdered!'" But he told Rice that he thought it was strange. How would Hawkenberry know Schultz had been murdered unless he was in the room and investigated? Although his room was next to Schultz's, Hawkenberry had no time to do either.

Schultz only had a twenty-dollar bill in his bloody vest, and his watch was found hidden under his pillow. No other money was found. Where had the money from the six months of work gone? Schultz was clad only in his undershirt, so he had obviously been sleeping at the time of the intrusion. Buttons were ripped and strewn about his room, suggesting a struggle.

One of the most incriminating aspects of the case was that, after the shots had been heard, Hawkenberry went outside, where he lingered for over five minutes. Rice suspected this was to dispose of (or hide) the gun.

The housekeeper for the Kaiser, Mrs. Mary Dolan, told Rice, "The two men adjacent to Schultz's room disappeared right after the murder."

ANOTHER CLUE WOULD SEND Hawkenberry to the slammer. Claude LeForce, a cook at the Headlight restaurant in town, told Rice that just a few days

Spokane's very first chief of police, Peter Mertz (*left*), in 1891, sitting with Inspector Phillip Gough. Mertz once worked as the conductor of a streetcar. *SPL/NWR.*

before the murder, Hawkenberry had tried to trade him his .32 revolver for his .38-caliber gun.

Rice promptly arrested Hawkenberry for the murder of Perry Schultz.

While in jail awaiting trial, Hawkenberry confided in his cell mate, Harry Palmer. He wrote a note to Gregg asking him to "go to cache and get the gun and money and secrete the gun."

That sealed the deal for Officer Rice.

After a two-week trial, Hawkenberry was found guilty of the murder of Perry Schultz and sentenced to one to twenty years in prison.

Schultz's body was sent back to Waukesha, Illinois, to be buried by his family. The stolen money and hidden gun were never found.

CHAPTER 3

SENSELESS MURDERS

Nobody's ever been arrested for a murder;
they have only ever been arrested for not planning it properly.
——*Terry Hayes,* I Am Pilgrim

DEATH OVER A DOLLAR

The murder of a man named Dusty Dean was about as senseless as they get. The end of a long-term friendship was complicated by the loaning of money that was never paid back. Some records indicate it was ten dollars; other records state it was only one dollar. To take a friend's life over a dollar? Seems ridiculous, and yet it happened one cold night on October 20, 1907.

The evening started off well, as friends Dusty Dean (1876–1907) and Robert Gray entered the Favorite Saloon on the corner of Front and Post Streets in Spokane, where one of their good friends was the proprietor. Eager for a cold beer and a shot of whiskey, the men made their way to the bar to drink together. Sometime later that evening, proprietor George W. Ragsdale (1871–1949) also began drinking. Dusty Dean and Ragsdale began to quarrel and took matters into the back room of the tavern. Not long after, Dean came stumbling back out to the bar with his face all bloody. About a half-dozen men stood in silence as Dean simply looked at them and then fell face first to the floor, unconscious.

Apparently, Ragsdale had lost his temper and hit Dean a few times in the face.

Post Street as seen from First Street toward Sprague Avenue, with Davenport Hotel and Cutter Studios on the left, Anderson Hotel and Acme Paints on the right. *SPL/NWR.*

As Dean lay motionless on the floor of the saloon, others quickly contacted Sergeant McPhee and Patrolman Daniel, who showed up in their patrol wagon. As soon as they entered the bar and saw Dean, they could tell he was already dead.

Ragsdale slowly walked out from the back room and approached the police.

He calmly told McPhee, "You had better take him to a hospital right away. He seems to be pretty bad off."

The two officers looked at one another, then back at Ragsdale. McPhee said, "It's too late now. The man is dead."

Ragsdale replied, "Well, then I suppose you want me."

They handcuffed the drunken Ragsdale and loaded him into the wagon.

When they questioned him, he told the cops his version of the story. "I struck him, but not hard enough to cause his death. I am crippled and incapable of striking hard. He has owed me money for several years and when he asked me for more, we had some words, which culminated in a fight. It is very unfortunate." He explained that a few years prior to owning the Favorite Saloon, he owned a tent saloon in Trout Creek, Montana. When a brutal fight broke out and fifty bullets were fired, Ragsdale was shot and became partially paralyzed. He had come to Spokane in 1905 and purchased the Favorite Saloon.

RAGSDALE WAS PLACED BEHIND bars and awaited his trial. Coroner Witter performed an autopsy on Dean at Smith's Undertaking and concluded that he had suffered from a deep gash on the side of his head, a hemorrhage of the brain and a busted artery at the base of his skull.

A tragic scene with countless unidentified soldiers during the Boer War, 1889–1902, when almost thirty thousand men died. *Library of Congress (LOC).*

Police Chief Rice soon received a letter in the post from a Mrs. W.S. Ross of Winnipeg, Canada. She claimed Dusty Dean was her brother. She wrote that he had served in the Boer War in South Africa. Dean had originally come from British Columbia. He had also been working as a railroad laborer.

The trial began for Ragsdale, and eventually he was convicted of involuntary manslaughter and sentenced to one to twenty years in prison by Judge Sullivan. Ragsdale went into foreclosure on the Favorite Saloon and lost it.

It would seem that just loaning his friend another dollar would have been a lot less hassle than ending up in prison for murder!

KILLED FOR A COUPLE OF HORSES

Horses and mules were extremely valuable in the old days, as their presence on a farm ensured valuable labor for the owner. If a man was riding on the open range and his horse was stolen from him, he would most likely die from exposure to the elements. Due to the severity of the consequences involved, the sentence for horse-stealing was hanging until death.

An early photograph of the Nine Mile Bridge. The body of local farmer Nes Cole was found near the bridge in 1906. *Washington State Archives, Spokane Municipal Government, Historic Preservation.*

One man, Charles Philpot (also known as Charles Williams, John Philpott, Will Meyers, Will Dodson), decided that stealing a man's horses was not enough; he'd better murder him too, just in case. Philpot was not new to trouble; he was arrested in 1904 for robbing thirty-five dollars from a man and again in 1906 for smoking opium with Sing Kee of the Poppy Palace on Wall Street in Spokane.

The Spokane headlines soon announced that Nes Cole, a sixty-eight-year-old rancher, had disappeared on March 28, 1906. He lived as a hermit in a small cabin at the mouth of the Little Spokane River, just ten miles from Spokane, and pretty much kept to himself. J.R. Tomey, also a farmer below Nine Mile Bridge, was one of the last men to see Cole alive. The men were friends, and Tomey had spent the night at Cole's the evening before his disappearance. Tomey told officers, "Cole was offered $300 for his team of horses, and he was wanting to buy the Gannon ranch. He told me that his wife liked the ranch and that he had walked the painstaking twenty-two miles round trip to Spokane and back just to see it for her. That was the last time I ever saw him."

Detectives were eager to figure out where Cole went. A suspicious note was pinned to Cole's cabin door that read:

I cannot plow, I am going out of town.

But something was fishy. Cole's horse team was gone, and his mattress and tent were thrown onto the porch. Why would he put his bed and tent on the porch if he was just going into town?

The mystery of his whereabouts wouldn't last long.

A month later, Cole's decomposed body was found by a rancher named Krum, floating in the Spokane River, twenty miles downstream. The victim's head had been beaten beyond recognition. He was identified by the sweater he was wearing.

Sheriff Doak took the note to the Old National Bank where Cole kept his money. Cashier W. Vincent analyzed the handwriting on the crumpled piece of paper. He said the handwriting was not that of Mr. Cole. He was certain.

If it wasn't Cole's handwriting, then whose was it?

Cole's team of horses was soon located too, in Coeur d'Alene, by William Tamlin. He told Marshall McGovern that he had purchased the team from a man named Charles Williams for $300 on March 30. He gave the sheriff the receipt as evidence. When E.F. Timberman of Blair Business College analyzed the note and the receipt, he concluded that the two were definitely the same handwriting, but again, not that of Cole. Whoever forged the note pinned to the cabin door was the same man who sold the team of horses to the Coeur d'Alene horse trader.

Back at Cole's farm, Deputy Hamlin discovered some wagon tracks. The tracks led through the canyon down toward Nine Mile Bridge, where the body was found. He also believed that there was no blood found at the Cole ranch because the chickens had eaten it.

The investigators immediately began searching for the man named Charles Williams who had sold Cole's team. Their hard work and detective skills led them to a farm in Freeman, Washington. There they found Philpot stacking hay in a field. He was promptly arrested for murder in the first degree of Nes Cole. The criminal denied he was a horse thief or a murderer and asserted his innocence.

Later he admitted he was a horse thief but insisted he would never murder anyone. He told the deputy he believed Cole's horses were sold by a man named Flood.

No one believed him, as he had already lied. His trial was set.

THE POLICE SOON HEARD more news from a few concerned citizens. They told the officers that, just the year before, a couple disappeared who also lived near Nine Mile Bridge. The concerned citizens had heard through the grapevine that their team of horses was also sold by Philpot to a trader named Wilson in Spokane. They had also heard that the mysterious couple met Philpot while traveling from Coeur d'Alene to Spokane. Philpot now became the prime suspect in other murders.

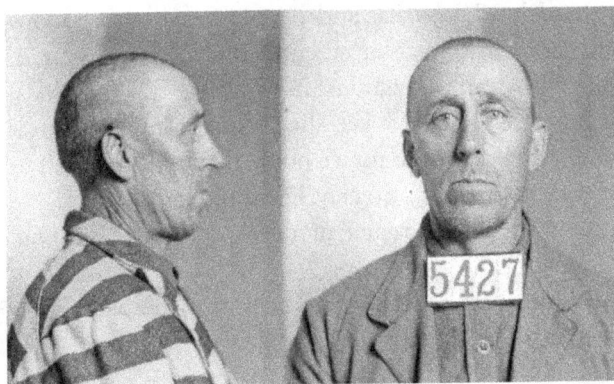

Charles Philpot was executed at the Walla Walla State Penitentiary for killing Nes Cole in 1906. *WSA.*

The killer's wife and his son, Otto, were devastated by the arrest.

Judge Carey sentenced Philpot to be hanged until death on April 19, 1906. Philpot still claimed he was innocent. Several appeals were filed, but all were denied. His family had to suffer for another three years while his attorney tried to get his sentence reduced. But he was sentenced to death a second time, and the hanging was scheduled for August 2, 1909. When the judge asked Philpot if he had anything to say, the killer simply mumbled, "None."

Charles Philpot was executed as scheduled at the Walla Walla State Penitentiary.

Note: Charles Philpot would walk side by side shackled to another ruthless Spokane killer named Joe Gauvette. On August 2, they walked through the front entrance of the county jail on Mallon Avenue and were led to the OR&N railroad depot to be taken by train to the Walla Walla State Penitentiary, where they would both be hanged.

A DEATH OVER SEX

On a freezing November night in 1899, near Fort George Wright, a man's life was taken tragically. William Freundt had heard rumors that his wife was having sex with another man named August Zaspel. Freundt was the local butcher, and he had had enough of his wife's affair. One night, he hid behind a tree, clutching his trusty Winchester rifle to his chest. When Zaspel walked past him, he quickly raised his gun and shot him! He then hid Zaspel's body under a few branches and went back home to go to bed.

The next day, Freundt went back to the murder site and buried the corpse in a shallow grave.

Soon, Zaspel was missed by the locals, and people became suspicious of foul play. Everyone in town knew that Freundt was a jealous man, embarrassed by his wife's extramarital relationship with Zaspel. When Mrs. Freundt found out that he had killed her lover, she was devastated. Freundt led her back to where he had hidden the man's body. He suddenly tried to deny what he had done, but then, just as quickly, he admitted his guilt.

Freundt was put in jail with a twenty-year sentence and a fifty-dollar fine, and he had to pay his own attorney costs.

Six months later, Freundt hanged himself in his cell out of despair.

THE BRUTAL MURDER OF GEORGE DANIELUK

Late one night in November 1908, a man's life would be taken brutally over a few bucks. The victim was George Danieluk, an Australian, who was considered by the citizens of Spokane to be a sober, well-liked, industrious and hardworking family man. He had a wife and three little children still living back home in Australia whom he was trying to support.

Normally, Danieluk would be hanging out at his favorite bar in Spokane, the Winnipeg Saloon on Stevens Street, with his favorite bartender, Joe Schultz. This particular night, November 9, he went to John Jahde's Saloon on the corner of Front and Division Streets for a change.

That was a mistake. It would end up being the last thing he ever did.

He was at the bar drinking casually with two men he just met, Mike Lockovitch and Drago Rakocevitch. Danieluk was getting pretty intoxicated, which was very unusual for him. Around 6:00 p.m., the three men began quarreling over something unknown. Soon the two men were carrying the staggering Danieluk out of Jahde's and into the street. With Danieluk in between them, Lockovitch and Rakocevitch held him up and dragged their victim to the corner of Front and Bernard Streets, about one hundred yards away.

Mike Lockovitch and Drago Rakocevitch stabbed to death George Danieluk on November 9, 1908, and left him for dead on Front Street. This photograph shows Front Street in 1888; several men are examining a large sinkhole on the right. *SPL/NWR.*

There the men proceeded to brutally beat up and stab poor Danieluk. He certainly put up a good fight, but in the end, he suffered a savage beating and seven mortal stab wounds. The men then quickly stole his wallet and ran out into the night.

The bloody corpse of George Danieluk was left in the middle of the road like a bag of garbage, on Ferry Avenue near the Great Northern Railroad freight house.

The next morning, his blood-drenched body was discovered by A.D. Gorham, a railroad engine foreman on his way to work.

Detectives McDermott and Herndon, as well as Coroner Witter, were called and quick to arrive at the scene. The men concluded that Danieluk was attacked from behind, as he had three deep stab wounds in his back, his right cheek was gashed and he had two more stab wounds in the neck and one in his arm. A ten-dollar bill and a quarter were still in his vest pocket, but his wallet was missing. There was also a letter from his wife in his vest pocket, easily identifying the victim. Coroner Witter was confident that Danieluk died from multiple hemorrhages resulting from the stab wounds.

The detectives began interviewing people near the area where the body was found.

The bartender at Jahde's, Joe Schultz, told the police that the Montenegrins (a South Slavic ethnic group native to Montenegro) who were drinking there that night had been giving Danieluk grief and bullying him.

Another witness was an out-of-work waiter named John Sullivan who came forward the next afternoon. As he read about the murder in the paper, he was shocked, because he knew he had seen the man just prior to his murder. He felt guilty; maybe he could have prevented it somehow. He quickly made his way to the morgue to see if the dead man was the same one he had seen the night before.

At the morgue, Coroner Witter met him at the door and Sullivan told him of his concerns. Witter led him to the back room.

The Great Northern Railroad depot and clock tower are backlit by the afternoon sun in this photograph by Frank Palmer. *SPL/NWR.*

"Did he wear glasses?" Sullivan asked Witter as they walked down the corridor.

Witter told the waiter, "Yes, the victim wore glasses." Sullivan then viewed the corpse and noted that it was definitely the man he had seen the night before being dragged into the railroad yard by two men.

Sullivan ran to the police station and told officers John McDermott and Thomas Herndon his story. He said that on the night of the murder, he went to the Great Northern Railroad yards to see if a train was leaving anytime soon. He was told that none were leaving until later that night, so he decided to walk back into town. As he walked away, he saw two men forcing a third man, who was obviously drunk, toward the railroad yards. As they walked past Sullivan, they both looked away, but Sullivan got a good look at the bigger of the two men. He noticed that the drunken man was wearing gold-rimmed glasses, was stocky and had a moustache.

Another witness was a Black man named W.C. Walker, who was a local cook at the train depot's restaurant. Although he lived on a nearby island, the night of the murder he had rowed back to town and boarded a coach to go to the depot. He, too, saw the men dragging the drunken man by his arms. He remembered them well, because they came right up to Walker and tried to intimidate him by calling him foul names. He positively identified Lockovitch as one of the men.

A third and very valuable witness was a nameless, homeless man. He saw the whole event unfold and was keen on helping the police catch the horrible killers. The detectives spent many days with this mysterious man, gathering clues and evidence against Lockovitch and his partner, Rakocevitch. As a star witness, he was willing to testify his claims in court, and this was disclosed in the local papers.

Unfortunately, the transient mysteriously went missing and the detectives feared he met with foul play so that he could not testify. They feared he was kidnapped and killed and his body hidden somewhere. Since he was a transient, no one would report him missing.

As the detectives continued to gather evidence to put Lockovitch and Rakocevitch behind bars, another tragedy occurred that stopped their progress. Detective McDermott (1854–1909) suddenly died on January 12. Much to everyone's surprise, including the killers', the case was dismissed because McDermott died before all of his findings could be entered into evidence to the court.

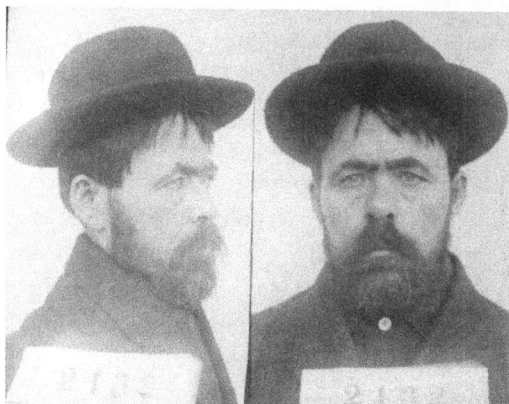

Borisa Rakocevitch was finally arrested in 1911 for the murder of George Danieluk. He had fled to Alaska to elude officers. *USP/ MNI.*

Another detective would soon take over the case, but as of January 1909, Lockovitch was still a free man.

Killer Rakocevitch was not as lucky. After he killed Danieluk, he tried to escape by catching the steamer SS *Princess May* on March 3, 1909. He got away for a while, hiding out in Alaska, but the never-tiring police continued their search for him. He was finally captured on December 18, 1991, in Fairbanks, Alaska, and taken back to McNeil Island prison, where he would become inmate #2132 and be sentenced to twenty-five years for murder in the second degree. He was forty years old. His real name was Borisa M. Rakocevitch.

The Mad Doctor of Spokane Gets Murdered

In the end, the "Mad Doctor of South Hill," Rudolf Albert Hahn (1865–1946), seems to have gotten a secret revenge when he was murdered in his own home with his own weapon.

His life story is an odd one—as odd as his own gruesome murder.

Hahn purchased his Spokane mansion in 1924 from a Spokane pharmacist named William T. Whitlock, who had only lived in the house for five years. Whitlock had purchased the home on Nineteenth Avenue from Rahlson and Sarah Wilbur, who built the home in 1916 using her deceased husband John Smith's money when he died in 1908. The Craftsman-style home was built on the side of a hill and lavishly adorned with massive stonework, huge boulders, a Japanese meditation garden, mother-of-pearl inlays, a beautiful arched stone bridge, intricately carved doorways (with a vine pattern painted in gold leaf) and four large Chinese lanterns in the living room. The house was situated on a little over three acres on South Hill. But all of this elegant luxury did not make the couple happy, and they divorced soon after the construction of the home was complete.

HAHN, A SELF-ABSORBED AND eccentric man from Chicago, married a twenty-one-year-old girl named Sylvia D. Fly (1898–1940) in 1933. Throughout the marriage, Hahn bullied Sylvia and enjoyed scaring her. Although he was technically licensed, he never really went to medical school to be a doctor. His preferred choice of medical services was performing illegal abortions and providing electroshock therapy to his patients. He also spent lots of money to build an underground tunnel from his home to the nearby garage—so his patients could enter the home in privacy for their "treatments" and stay out of the public's leering eyes.

Hahn was known to throw extravagant and drunken parties during which he would play ridiculously loud music, to the irritation of his neighbors. He wore absurdly expensive suits, while his feet were clad in mere bedroom slippers. One of the most bizarre habits he had? He would shoot his guns inside the home. His target? Insects.

Then one day in 1940, his wife supposedly committed suicide in the home.

The investigating officers found that the interior walls were riddled with bullet holes when they arrived that fateful May 2, 1940, after Hahn called them to report the death of his wife.

The police found poor Sylvia dead in her bed with a gunshot wound to her head. Apparently, Sylvia had a history of suicidal threats, but did she really go through with it this time? It was noted in the coroner's report that there was some evidence of gunshot residue on her hands. As the *Evening Star* reported on May 7, the coroner concluded that Mrs. Hahn was indeed killed by a "self-inflicted gunshot wound."

It took only thirty-eight minutes for the jurors to decide it was suicide. Sylvia was forty-two years old at the time of her death, and Hahn was seventy-four. Hahn testified under oath that he had "heard the doorbell then heard a gunshot and ran to find his wife dead."

HAHN SOLD THE HOME in 1945 because he felt he could not live in the home anymore without his wife. His life got worse when a patient from Mullan, Idaho, died on his operating table after he performed one of his illegal abortions. He was charged with manslaughter and became involved in a complicated legal matter. Although he was found guilty, he was only ordered to "no longer practice medicine." Since Hahn was eighty-one years old, the judge just gave him a fine and placed him on probation—clearly, he was too old to put in jail.

Hahn moved into the New Madison Hotel in Spokane, located on the corner of First and Madison. A year later, on August 6, 1946, Hahn innocently answered the door to his apartment to find a hearing aid salesman named Delbert Visger standing there. The true story will never be known, but a fight ensued and somehow Visger got ahold of one of Hahn's World War II bayonets and stabbed him in the heart. Some believe the stabbing was revenge for a botched abortion that Hahn performed on a loved one of Visger's a few years before. How many other victims died at Hahn's hands? If by chance Hahn was killed by a salesman he didn't even know, the murder was truly senseless.

A MURDER-SUICIDE AT THE PEDICORD HOTEL

Mark McClammy was a Coeur d'Alene resident whose life took a tragic and horrific turn for the worse.

The story starts a year before the murder-suicide affair, when the couple was married in Eddy, New Mexico, in 1897. The abuse suffered by Etta McClammy during their marriage began on Thanksgiving Day in 1903 and continued to worsen as the years went by.

In 1907, Mr. McClammy purchased a small house from P.T. Nixon, located on the corner of Ninth and Wallace Streets in Coeur d'Alene for $2,750, in the hopes of moving his family in and starting over.

But the McClammys were having marital difficulties that the wife felt were beyond repair, which were coupled with her complete lack of desire to make the marriage work.

The couple had moved to Coeur d'Alene from Sandpoint in the hopes that a change could invigorate their love for one another, but it did not work. Mr. McClammy was a notorious gambler and was known to be abusive to his wife. Proprietor Doc Brown would testify that he was a regular at his Owl Saloon in Spokane. Mrs. McClammy fell in front of the Mott Block in Spokane the year before and sued the city for damages. She won the case, and soon the couple was $7,000 richer. Mr. McClammy took half of the money and, returning to Sandpoint, desired to open a gambling hall, but that line of work would only increase his drinking and gambling problems. Luckily, the deal fell through.

When he would become intoxicated, Mr. McClammy would threaten to kill his wife. A restraining order was finally put into effect.

The terrified Mrs. McClammy promptly left him again and returned to the safety of Coeur d'Alene. She was tired of his drama and filed for a divorce after his final threat on New Year's Day in 1908. She was soon sitting in the lawyer's offices of Black, Wernette and E.N. LaVeine. Mr. McClammy did not take to the divorce kindly and threatened to kill her if she followed through with the suit. He also threatened to kill her lawyers.

Running for her life again, on January 19 she packed her things and decided to move herself, her five-year-old daughter, Eva, and their eight-year-old son, Harold, to a room on the third floor of the Pedicord Hotel in Spokane, hoping to hide away there until the divorce was final. Without looking back, they boarded the last train from Coeur d'Alene to Spokane, hoping to finally get some much-needed peace from the troublesome situation.

On January 20, in retaliation for Etta's filing for divorce, Mr. McClammy quickly marched over to Sheriff McGovern's office and demanded Etta be arrested on the grounds of the embezzlement of $750 and the abduction of the children.

For some reason, Judge Steele signed off on the ridiculous charges, and Etta was found by the police and arrested at the Pedicord Hotel in Spokane. She was later cleared of the charges.

The tension between the couple continued. Although Etta tried to surround herself with her friends for safety, her plan did not work.

On February 16, as soon as Mr. McClammy found out his wife's whereabouts, he, too, rented a room at the Pedicord Hotel. He tried to reconcile with his wife daily; she desperately wanted no part of this. More threats by him followed.

Perhaps Etta should have taken his rants about killing her more seriously...

On the afternoon of February 23, his horrific threats became a reality. After talking things over for more than an hour in the hallway of the hotel, McClammy began to finally realize he was never going to be able to persuade his wife to return to him. In a huff, he stormed off down the hall.

Etta quickly closed the door, hoping that was the end of it.

But it wasn't.

The angry Mark McClammy, wielding a .38-caliber pistol, marched back over to her room, the gun hidden in his waistcoat. He demanded she open the door once again for him.

When she answered the door, he asked her again if she would return to him, and she simply replied, "No, I will not."

This was the last time Etta would argue with her husband.

Their frightened young son stood silently nearby witnessing the horrible arguing between his parents.

Frustrated, Mark commented to Etta, "Well then, this ends *everything* between us," and quickly drew his concealed gun.

Etta had no time to retreat or close the door.

Without hesitation, he calmly shot his wife four times.

The hotel's maid, Lucy Smith, stood nearby frozen in fear, then immediately ran down the stairs screaming at the top of her lungs for help. The insane Mr. McClammy then turned the gun on himself, pointing the weapon precisely at his right temple, and pulled the trigger—killing himself instantly.

The surprised hotel help soon arrived at the bloody scene. They carefully assisted Mrs. McClammy to her bed then quickly called for a doctor and the police.

The Spokane police arrived and immediately called for the undertaker to come to the Pedicord Hotel; it was obvious Mr. McClammy was 100 percent dead. His body was taken to the Buchanan morgue in Spokane.

The doctor and nurse arrived and ran to Etta's bedside, hoping to give her some relief or somehow save her.

They concluded that Etta had suffered from three of the four gunshots; one bullet hit her liver, a second pierced below her heart and a third shattered her wrist. The doctor and nurse shook their heads in unison; sadly, she would not live through the attack.

The two horrified small children stood near their dying mother, forever traumatized by the entire scenario.

Etta soon fell into a coma. The physician made her comfortable with an injection of morphine. For the next hour, Etta moved in and out of consciousness.

At one point, she was clear enough to tell her nurse, "Please don't let me die yet. I want to see a minister. Keep me alive as long as you can."

The good Reverend C. William Giboney of the nearby Presbyterian church rushed to her bedside and offered his help. Etta begged him to baptize her. As soon as the reverend completed his impromptu baptism, she fell back into a coma.

Little Eva came to her mother's bedside and sat silently. She held a ripe orange, in the hopes of giving the fruit to her mom. Etta seemed to waken for just a moment and smiled at her daughter. It was the last time the two would interact.

Then a nurse came to her bedside to check on her bandages. Etta reached for the woman's hand and quietly told the lady, "I know the end is near, and under *no* circumstances is my body to be buried next to that of my husband!" The nurse and reverend nodded and reassured the dying woman that her final request would be honored.

Etta died at 4:48 p.m. on February 24 at the Pedicord Hotel from her gunshot wounds.

SOON, THE BODIES OF both Mr. and Mrs. McClammy lay together in the morgue at Buchanan's.

The brother of Mr. McClammy, known only as R.P., arrived from Montana to take control of the children. Other references tell that the children went to live with the Boone family in California.

Both of the bodies are buried in Spokane, but as promised, the two lie apart in eternal peace.

Etta was only thirty-eight years old at the time of her murder. It is a very sad and unfortunate outcome, as the restraining order to protect her life was in place but obviously not enforced by local authorities. After suffering years of abuse, she simply wanted to move on from her married life and create a safe and loving environment for herself and her two small children.

Yet her life was cut short in the most horrible manner: at the hands of a man she (at one time) loved and trusted enough to marry.

THE BROOKS AND DOHLMAN MURDER

The first person to be legally hanged in Spokane was a sixty-two-year-old Black man named Charles Brooks, who murdered his estranged wife, twenty-seven-year-old Christine Dohlman, in cold blood.

Brooks was formerly enslaved in Mississippi, before the Civil War. He suffered from a head injury from a bullet that he received while serving in the Colored Regiment of Tennessee. Some attribute his murderous action to this brain injury. Others do not.

BROOKS FELL IN LOVE and asked Christine for her hand in marriage after only a few weeks of courting. Brooks promised Christine a life of wealth and happiness. Although he was barely making a living as a janitor at the

Webster house, he told her he had over $30,000 in Spokane real estate and could provide a nice life for them. Brooks *did* hold money in real estate, but unfortunately, since he was illiterate, he had been cheated out of his land claims in 1888 by his son-in-law (whom Brooks shot in the neck in a rage after he found out about the incident).

Christine soon found out the truth about Brooks's financial woes and his violent temper.

Frustrated that she had been so misled and lied to, she filed for a divorce from Brooks in June 1891. The angry Brooks began threatening to kill her if she didn't return to him.

After Christine announced to Brooks that she was still going through with the divorce, he became even more violent and unpredictable, but she was determined to move on with her life.

ONE SUMMER EVENING, JULY 5, 1891, Christine and her sister got together and decided to take a stroll. Brooks silently followed behind the women. He continued to follow Christine and her sister, Mrs. Moline (who also had her two children with her, keep in mind), as they were walking along the alley by the Penobscot Hotel on Havermale Island.

Brooks rushed up behind the women, startling and frightening them both.

The *Seattle-Post Intelligencer* told the story on September 7: Brooks approached Christine and said, "I want to speak with you!" Christine replied, "I don't want anything to do with you!" As the two women and the children turned to walk away, Brooks pulled out his revolver and shot his wife in the back of the head. Then he fired another two shots at her. As Christine fell to the ground, she was still cradling one of her sister's children. The screaming Mrs. Moline hurriedly grabbed her child from her dying sister's arms and fled the scene.

Brooks was reported to be calm and just remained standing over his wife's dead body.

Officer William Smith was patrolling nearby and, when he heard the shots, went running to the area, where he saw the grisly scene. When he asked Brooks what had happened, Brooks remained calm, the gun still in his hand.

Brooks quietly said, "You can take me and hang me now," which Spokane County was definitely prepared to do.

Brooks was tried and convicted in October 1891 of murdering his wife. His lawyer appealed on the grounds of insanity, due to his head injury. His appeal was denied by the Supreme Court, and he was sentenced to the gallows.

Sheriff Francis K. Pugh sent out 150 formal invitations to the citizens of Spokane to attend Brooks's hanging, which was scheduled for September 6, 1892, at the Spokane Courthouse. In that era it was, strangely, considered an honor to be invited to a public execution. When word got out, over one thousand citizens crowded to the event, although they were not allowed inside the fence to actually see the hanging.

It was reported that Brooks was calm prior to the event; he even participated in the singing of "When I Can Read My Title Clear." Then he smoked a cigar while walking on the path to his death trap. After the hood was placed over his head and the clock struck the designated time, the trap was released, and Brooks died instantly.

The strange part of the story is that Brooks is buried in an unmarked grave (no one offered to buy a plot or headstone for him) at Spokane's Greenwood Memorial Terrace, and the poor body of Christine Dohlman was for some reason buried next to him for all eternity.

Insane Man Kills His Wife

Joe Gauvette had a long history of mental illness, but family and officials didn't seem to take it seriously. That is, until he brutally killed his wife.

On that fateful afternoon of June 24, 1908, Mrs. Elizabeth Gauvette came home from her day of grocery shopping and casual errands. A frantic Joe Gauvette was eagerly waiting for her return, in a mad craze, believing his wife was having an extramarital affair. No matter how many times in the past Elizabeth had tried to reassure Joe that she was faithful, he did not believe her. Elizabeth had done everything she could do to try to save herself from his insanity. Three weeks before he killed her, she had filed for both a restraining order *and* a divorce. She told authorities that she feared for her life and that he had threatened to kill her many times. She claimed he was insane and requested that he be locked up for her protection until the divorce was final and the restraining order was in place.

But they did not lock him up.

Pleading for safety from him was the last thing Elizabeth ever did.

That day, Gauvette shot down his wife in front of their house, in front of multiple witnesses.

Joe Gauvette was the proprietor of the Bodega Saloon in Spokane, on the corner of Monroe Street and College Avenue. An employee named H.E. Kidney told the police that "Gauvette had a weird laugh...an *inhuman* laugh."

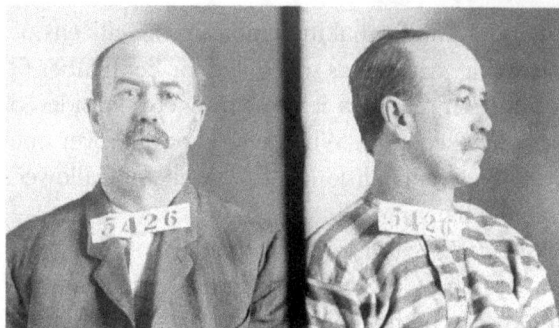

Joe Gauvette was hanged for killing his wife, Elizabeth, in 1908. *Washington State Archives, Corrections Department, Washington State Penitentiary, Commitment Registers and Mug Shots, 1887–1946 (WSA/CD).*

But having a weird laugh did not necessarily mean you were a cold-blooded killer.

Frank Hatton, who would later buy the bar from Gauvette, told the police, "Gauvette would crawl around on the floor of the saloon, under the tables, making weird gestures and knocking over bar glasses. He was a real bug house!"

Another person, Earnest Otis, who knew Gauvette, said he had a "shaky look and a ferocious appearance."

When arrested by Sheriff McPhee, Gauvette remained calm and coolheaded.

During the trial, his attorneys, Justin and Moore, immediately went for the insanity plea for the murder of his wife. While alive, she had filed charges and said herself that he was insane during her divorce proceedings, so that made it easy for his lawyers.

The jury, witnesses, officers and judge were all astonished when Gauvette's brother from Minneapolis, W.C., took the stand. What he told them was bone-chilling. "Joe assaulted our dad with a monkey wrench, and he wanted me to hold our father's head so he could chop it off!" He also disclosed that five members of their mother's side of the family were all insane. It ran in the family. "He has been for years more or less crazy and has always doubted his wife's honor. The insanity of my brother is hereditary and comes from my mother's side."

When the distraught wife of W.C. took the stand, she told them, "If we had known that Joe was in as bad of a mental condition as we learned he was, we would have come to Spokane to help and have done something to protect his family." Joe and Elizabeth had one child, Florence, who was age twelve when he killed her mother.

Experts believed Gauvette was crazy and should be committed to an insane asylum, not be hanged for murder.

Ten witnesses testified that they felt Gauvette was perfectly sane when he killed his wife.

The angry Gauvette announced to the courtroom, "I don't care what they do to me in this case, just so they tell the truth. It gets me nervous and excited when they tell a lot of lies. If I am to hang for this, I want to be hung after a fair trial!"

After much consideration by the jury, Judge J.D. Hinkle revealed the sentence they provided. He said, "In view of the jury, we found the defendant, Joseph M. Gauvette, to be mentally responsible at the time he killed his wife. It is therefore the judgement of the court that the defendant be executed by hanging by the neck until dead."

On June 4, 1909, Judge Hinkle requested him to be moved to the Walla Walla State Penitentiary.

Joe Gauvette was allowed to see his sweet little daughter the night before his hanging and bid her farewell.

At 5:30 a.m. on June 29, he was led to the scaffold, where he wept. Joe Gauvette's final words were, "I have no hard feelings toward anyone."

Next, the trap was sprung, and his neck was instantly broken.

THE STATE WAS BILLED $1,750 for the nine doctors who examined Gauvette: $25 per exam and $25 each per day of the trial. It was considered the most expensive case since the trial of Sidney Sloane, conducted several years before in Spokane.

A Spokane Serial Killer Gets Caught

Perhaps one of the most gruesome murders in Spokane's history is that of an innocent young girl named Kelly Conway.

Forty-six-year-old convicted killer Stanley Pietrzak was charged with Kelly's murder and possibly killed two others. Conway's disappearance went unnoticed for some time, until concerned citizens and fellow tenants in Kelly's building finally got brave enough to go to the police. By coming forward, they were able to bring justice for his victim and possibly save other people from suffering the same terrible fate.

Working as the manager of the apartments on the northeast corner of Adams Street and Second Avenue from 1997 to 1998, Pietrzak lured victim Kelly Conway into his apartment. Conway was partially disabled and lived in the apartment building. A small group would occasionally get together to drink and watch TV. The night of Kelly's death, she was complaining of a backache. Pietrzak offered her some pills to relieve her pain. The others finally went back to their own apartments, leaving Conway to her untimely and unfortunate demise.

Conway was last seen alive that November night in 1998. No one knew where she had vanished for almost a year.

In the spring of 1999, police got a tip to search the basement for Conway's remains. Apparently, Pietrzak had been bragging about killing her and even went so far as professing cannibalism. He told several people that Kelly was "better off dead." This, too, got back to the police. The police quickly arrested Pietrzak.

After he was convicted of first-degree murder, Pietrzak testified that he did not kill her but simply "woke up and found her dead in his bed." He panicked, and after a few days, he reportedly dismembered her body and burned her in the basement furnace. But the evidence found in the basement told another story—one so horrible it is hard to comprehend.

Police were positive that Pietrzak had strangled and killed Conway, then dismembered her body (after hiding it for a week) and proceeded to burn it in the basement's furnace. In April 1999, acting on a tip, police searched the building's basement and found a piece of her scalp with attached hair hanging from a gas line and her bones inside an old furnace. Investigating police were able to match some remaining hair from the furnace with DNA logged from Conway during a surgery prior to her murder. This evidence sealed Pietrzak's guilt. He finally admitted that he had dragged Conway's body to the basement, where he removed her head and hands with a serrated knife. Then he placed the head and hands in a garbage sack that he dumped into a passing garbage truck. Later, he burned the rest of the body in the furnace. The police also discovered a walk-in freezer that was made into a makeshift torture chamber down in the basement of the building. They feared that Pietrzak was responsible for several other local disappearances of women as well.

After the autopsy, forensic pathologist Dr. George Lindholm ruled Conway's death an absolute homicide. Pietrzak was sentenced to a mere forty years, and the system suffered his many appeals.

It is interesting to note that Karen Pietrzak, Stanley Pietrzak's former wife, died in a suspiciously similar manner in his bed in 1976. Another woman, Allison Weaver, was also found dead in his bed in 1998. Coincidence? Not likely.

Some felt Pietrzak should have gotten life in prison without parole, or just been hanged like in the old days.

The apartment building is now being beautifully renovated. It is a relief to know Pietrzak is locked up and cannot hurt any more innocent women. In August 2000, he was sentenced to serve forty years in jail.

DEAD DEPUTY FOUND IN SPOKANE RIVER

William Cook was a Spokane deputy who went mysteriously missing for two months. He was last seen at the State Armory Hall at 202 West Second Street on January 21, 1909. It was noted that he had fifteen dollars in his wallet. Cook was a reliable employee and had no known enemies.

Unfortunately, months later, his body was found by a man named Joe Heffner, floating in the river near the foot of Oak Street. Cook's coat and gold watch were missing, which suggested his death may have been brought on by robbery. They only found his identification and seventy-five cents on his body. Although Cook had suffered several wounds to his head, the coroner decided his death was actually due to drowning. His body was held at Gilman Undertaking until his funeral, and the killer was never found.

Perhaps Deputy Cook's killer was one of the men who, at the Cooks' home earlier that year, proceeded to fight with Mr. and Mrs. Cook under the influence of alcohol. It was reported in the *Spokane Press* that Jacob Hargert brawled with Cook and then gave the man several blows to his head with a hammer. The other man, Conrad Lind, tried to assault Mrs. Cook. The two men were charged with the assaults; maybe they took out their revenge on Cook for pressing charges and killed him?

Sadly, the world will never know the truth, and this case goes in the pile of unsolved Spokane murders.

FANTASTIC DUEL IN THE STREET

Robberies and pickpockets were very common in the early 1900s. Women were as guilty as men; they would honey up to a stranger, pretending to be attracted to him, yet all the while relieving him of his wallet. Night watchmen on patrol had to be constantly aware and suspicious of any activity that seemed out of place.

The dangerous job of a night watchman required much nerve. Sometimes they were armed with nothing more than a billy club and a whistle. *LOC.*

One night, on October 25, 1905, Spokane officer Jillsett had his skills tested as a fantastic shootout occurred and all chambers were emptied. Over twelve rounds were fired between the officer and three thugs on the corner of Sprague Avenue and Division Street. Nearby citizens ran in fear of getting hit by stray bullets and took cover wherever they could. Surprisingly, Jillsett did not get struck by any bullets, but he got a good shot at one of the robbers.

The night started out as any other at the Division Saloon, until a strange man slowly entered the bar. Saloon proprietor Peters was instantly on guard. The stranger looked him square in the eyes and said, "If I had a gun, I would hold up the whole ---- place!"

Peters, somewhat relaxed now, challenged him, holding out his gun to the man. The man just guffawed and stormed out of the bar. The men in the bar all had a laugh at that one.

Officer Jillsett was making his rounds as usual, and when he entered the Division Saloon, Peters told him what had happened earlier.

"I will keep a keen eye on the place tonight, just in case," Officer Jillsett told Peters, and continued on his patrol.

No strange activities happened all night. The Division Saloon closed as usual after last call.

But when the clock struck 3:00 a.m., things changed. As Jillsett passed by the Division Saloon, he noticed several men crouched inside, trying to break into the safe. One of the men said, "For God's sake, hurry up! Here comes that ------ policeman!"

Jillsett shot at the intruders, and shots were returned just as quickly.

A flurry of bullets went back and forth between the men for some time. Miraculously, Jillsett somehow remained safe from fire.

Earlier, a man named Frank Harvey had looked through the window and seen the men trying to get the safe open. Instead of notifying police headquarters, he ran down Sprague until he found a night watchman named Officer McQuillan. McQuillan quickly went to the scene and also shot at the robbers, but by then the robbers were out of sight. If Harvey had contacted the headquarters, it's possible that they could have surrounded the place and arrested the thieves.

Unknown men pose in an unknown bar for a photograph. Saloons like this one were common on the streets of Spokane. *WSA.*

City Hall & Police Headquarters - 1889.

Spokane policemen and city hall workers pose for a photograph in front of their headquarters in 1889. Fifth from the right is Moses "Mode" Harbord, chief of police in 1890, and on the far right is Captain John Sullivan, who served twenty-one years until his assassination in 1911. *WSA.*

When the Division Saloon was searched, the officers noted that the robbers had entered the saloon through a back window. They ransacked the register and, finding nothing in it, took a large hammer to the safe. Here they lucked out, for the safe had a whopping $329.20 in it.

The Division Saloon had blood all over the place. Even the proprietor's dog got involved in the shootout and apparently got his teeth into one of the men. Bloody paw prints mingled with boot prints leading out into the sidewalk and street. The officers followed the bloody prints, but eventually they petered out. The dog was never found.

THE ROBBERS HAD BEEN busy that night, as the police came to find out. How the watchmen did not stumble upon the other robberies is unknown.

The Ideal Laundry was hit, and the men trashed the cash register in hopes of acquiring loot. It was empty. So was the safe.

The frustrated men took to the next place, the East End Grocery Store at 30 East Sprague Avenue. Here the thugs broke the glass window in the door to gain entrance. Inside they found a mere fifty cents in the till. The safe held twelve dollars, which they took. Oddly, they also helped themselves to six bottles of Lea & Perrins pepper sauce.

Next they hit up the East End Butcher Shoppe, next door to the grocery. The register had twenty cents left in it. The men decided they would not leave empty-handed, so they went shopping instead. They gathered meat, a few dozen eggs, sixteen strips of bacon and ten pounds of sausage. They put these items in a basket, probably to retrieve later that night.

The robbers were never captured.

KILLED OVER A FREE MEAL

Although he had plenty of money, John (James) McDermott (also known as McDermitt or Watson) decided he wanted a free meal one night at a local café. He picked the Central Café, located at 6 Howard Street in Spokane, for his adventure. An innocent victim, the café's proprietor, Otis DeLacey, wanted no part of Watson's shenanigans that evening on July 21, 1905.

When McDermott shuffled into the restaurant, he asked DeLacey to "stand him off" for a meal, suggesting he wanted the man to give him a free dinner. With a gruff refusal and a quick "I can do nothing for you," DeLacey asked him to leave the establishment and continued on about his business.

But McDermott would not go away quietly. He decided to return to the Central Café, this time with a revolver. He quickly raised his gun and aimed it directly at DeLacey. Before DeLacey could even react, the gun was fired three times and two of the bullets were lodged in his upper torso.

Running from his assailant, DeLacey moved from the front saloon area to the back kitchen space. The café's pantry man, L.W. Purffley, was coming up from the cellar when all the commotion started. At the top of the stairs, he was trodden on by the bleeding man, and they both fell down the cellar stairs. DeLacey, confused and panicked, ran into the closet in the basement, where he tried to hide. "Don't let him shoot anymore," was all he said. He then got up and ran to the storeroom and sat down on a box.

"Are you hurt?" Purffley asked. Purffley was also now bleeding, as he had hit his head on the stairs when they fell.

"Yes," DeLacey mumbled, and he showed the man his wounds. He had been shot once in the left arm and shoulder area, and another bullet

In 1905, John McDermott shot and killed Otis DeLacey in his business, Central Café, at 6 Howard Street. This photograph shows Howard Street looking south from Front Street in 1888. *SPL/NWR.*

penetrated his chest above the breastbone. He tried to stand up but instantly fell on his face.

A brave woman named Rose Donofinet (also known as Rosa Donofino), who entered the café after the shooting, came to DeLacey's side and told him and Purffley, "*I* know who did it."

"It's *not* who you think," replied DeLacey. Those were the last words he spoke.

SOON, DETECTIVE MACDONALD WAS at the bloody scene. He arrested McDermott and hauled him off to the city jail. Once there, Chief of Police Waller began asking him why he shot and killed DeLacey. McDermott pretended to be drunk, staggering and slurring his words, but Waller knew he was bluffing. After a few more minutes of interrogating McDermott, the man broke down crying.

"Do you know that you are up against a pretty stiff proposition?" asked Waller.

"I don't know. All I can remember is that I was drinking some yesterday, not much, and then went to the hotel. There I decided to get one more drink. That's all I can remember until I found myself somewhere around here."

"When a man takes another man's life, that's taking something that's pretty hard to give back."

McDermott became nervous. "I didn't kill nobody, did I, Chief? That's awful. I have never been in trouble before. I can't understand it." He said he had no recollection of the entire incident. He was told that he almost killed a second man in his spree, the night cook for the café, as the third bullet missed him by a mere inch or two.

Watson then told the chief that he had come to Spokane from Butte, Montana, with sixty dollars in cash on him. He was a railroad man by trade. When the police made him empty his pockets, McDermott had $9.15 in cash and the revolver on him. It had been reported earlier that a man entered the pawnshop owned by C. Beckwith at Washington Street around 8:30 p.m. that same night and purchased a .38-caliber revolver. The shooting took place just two hours later.

DURING THE TRIAL, McDERMOTT looked solemn. He did not have the face of a cold-blooded killer. He quietly pled guilty to murder in the second degree to Spokane judge Poindexter.

The judge was astonished. It was the first time in Spokane's history that a man had actually acknowledged his crime and pled guilty to it.

The twenty-nine-year-old McDermott became inmate #3879 at the Washington State Penitentiary, where he was sentenced to ten years for killing Mr. DeLacey. While in jail, he was a model inmate, and everyone liked him.

WHAT IS INTERESTING IS that DeLacey's final words were "It's not who you think." Why would he even say that if everyone thought it was McDermott? Who was he referring to? Did someone else have a grudge against DeLacey and shoot him? Why would McDermott have absolutely no recollection of the incident? Did Rose Donofinet positively identify McDermott as the man's killer? Did the right man go to prison for the murder of DeLacey?

Upon investigation, the tragic tale does have more twists...

DeLacey's Lover, the Troubled Rose

The mysterious woman who came to DeLacey's side, Rose Donofinet (also known as Rosa Donofino), was actually his lover. She entered the café after the fatal shooting and told him and Purffley, "I know who did it."

Looking along Howard Street around 1890, with the Spokane & Eastern Trust Company building on the left. *SPL/NWR.*

Who was she talking about?

Rose had been troubled by a stalker named Louis Rapoli (also known as Louie Ripoli), an Italian shoemaker in Spokane, whose business was located on the corner of Howard Street and Second Avenue.

Rapoli had been harassing the poor girl for years, threatening to kill her if she did not marry him. She told him repeatedly that she was in love with Otis DeLacey, the proprietor of the Central Café. But Rapoli did not care; he was determined to make Rose his wife. He would follow her around day and night. He would stand in front of her house at 506½ Sprague Avenue and stare through her windows, watching her every move.

Rose, fearing for her life, told the police, "I don't think I will live very long. That man, Louis Rapoli, is crazy. I am afraid that if I say anything, he will kill me."

The chief of police, Leroy Waller, made sure Rapoli knew that if he even so much as harmed a hair on that girl's head, Waller would "make it warm" for him. Even the mayor of Spokane, F.L. Daggett, was hoping to help keep Rose safe: "I will do all in my power to afford protection for this unfortunate girl."

"Time and time again, he begs me to marry him and threatens to kill me. He can kill me, perhaps, but never will I marry him," Rose told reporters.

Rapoli was arrested in 1904 for slapping Mrs. Pauline Harris in the face. He had been arrested two times and sent to jail for harassing Rose. The first time he went to prison was for threatening to kill Rose, and the second time was for boxing her ears. Patrolman McQuillan tried to keep Rose safe, but Rapoli persisted in his desires.

A Second Stalker?

Rose told the police her story:

> I was born and raised in California from poor parents. I had a childhood friend named Tony Willardo, who was a relative of my sister in law's. Willardo wanted to marry me, but my parents objected. I moved to Tacoma to work as a maid for a family, and Willardo followed me there. He began threatening that if I did not marry him, he would kill me. That is when I met Otis DeLacey and fell in love with him. We were man and wife, even though we were not married yet. We lived together and wanted to save money to buy a house. We moved to Spokane. Willardo followed us there. He threatened to kill me and Otis. We had $190 saved up toward our house. Then Otis was shot! Immediately following his murder, Willardo began showering me with gifts and money, because I was almost penniless. I refused him and told him that even though DeLacey was gone, my love for him was forever and I would remain true. This infuriated Willardo. I found out he wanted to make me a slave, like the Claiche woman.

ROSE EVENTUALLY WENT INTO hiding from these men. It would make more sense that Otis DeLacey was actually murdered by one of these two crazy stalkers, rather than killed by James McDermott. Why would McDermott demand a free meal when he had $9.15 on him? Possibly he waved his gun around in a drunken rage, but was he mad enough to murder over a meal? Unlikely. And how would Rose have even known McDermott, since he was a stranger to the Central Café? If Rose did not know the killer, she would not have said, "I *know* who did it." Rose and DeLacey were recently engaged to be married, so either of the two crazy men would have had reason to kill DeLacey.

CHAPTER 4
DRUNKEN MURDERS

Murder is always a mistake. One should never do anything
that one cannot talk about after dinner.
—*Oscar Wilde*

SPOKANE'S HATCHET KILLER

The grisly, bloody bodies of several victims were found by authorities, all crammed into the tiny back room where a couple was living behind their sign shop. The East Side Sign Shop at 1806 East Sprague in Spokane was owned by Theodore Patrick Dillon (1905–1944) and his wife, Flora Gertrude (1910–1944).

The evening started out with the promise of a good time: a group of people hanging out in a bar, just drinking and having fun…

But that evening, the party came to a screeching halt as four people were attacked and three killed in the early morning hours by a hatchet-wielding drunken stranger.

ON JANUARY 14, 1944, everyone was having a good time at a local tavern in Spokane. Some records indicate it was the Sprague Street Tavern; others state it was the Rainbow Tavern. Either way, this is where the party started that would soon end in a drunken tragedy with three people dead.

The soon-to-be killer was a devilishly handsome twenty-seven-year-old man named Woodrow Wilson "Whitey" Clark (1916–1946). Clark was drinking alone when he met the Dillon couple, Jane Staples (1918–1944) and Frank Winnett (1912–1983), and a group of others at the bar. They were all friendly and having a good time together. When closing time came, the Dillons purchased more beer and moved the party to their house, next door. They were all clearly intoxicated already, but that didn't stop any of them from partying on.

The details of the evening were told to the police by Clark himself, after he was apprehended.

Clark's chilling confession went something like this (from court records):

On the evening of January 14, 1944, I went to a beer joint in Spokane, where I joined T.P. Dillon, Mrs. Dillon, Mrs. Jane Staples, Ed Johnson and Frank Winnett. After drinking beer at the place mentioned, we went to the Rainbow Tavern, which was next door to the Dillons' shop and residence. Jesse Hayford and Robert Hart then joined the party. At midnight the group, after purchasing several quarts of beer and a dozen eggs, went to the living quarters of the Dillons. After some more drinking, Dillon became angry with me because I was coming on to his wife. It was my intention that if Dillon left the house, I was going to go to bed with Mrs. Dillon.

About 2:00 a.m., Robert Hart went and got bacon from his apartment. I began building a fire, and we had a dinner (or early breakfast) of bacon and eggs. Most of us continued to drink beer. Hart fell asleep in his chair, awakening at 4:00 a.m., and then he, Johnson and Hayford left. Myself, Dillon, Mrs. Dillon, Frank Winnett and Mrs. Staples remained at the Dillon apartment. The parties went to bed. Mrs. Dillon was lying on the bed next to the wall, next to Mrs. Dillon was her husband, next to him was Mrs. Staples, and I was lying alongside her. During the early morning hours, I tried again to seduce and have sex with one of the two women. Everyone else was asleep. I do not know which one of the women I was trying to have sex with at that time. My efforts aroused Dillon, who attempted to arise from the bed, but I killed him with a hatchet. In a rage, I then killed the two women. When I started to leave the bedroom, Winnett started for me, and I hit him, and I left after that. I remember chopping wood for the stove and cooking a lot of bacon and eggs. After that, I was pretty drunk, and some of the guys got angry with me for making passes at their women. That's what made me mad. I waited until everyone but the four of them had left. They said they were tired and were going to take a nap. When they all fell asleep on the bed, I went into the kitchen, got the hatchet and beat them over the head with it. I don't know what made me do it.

But his story did not add up, possibly because he was too drunk to actually remember the details. Clark wrote and signed his confession without any fear and without threats or intimidations by the police. The real details of the night's massacre began to emerge from witnesses.

When questioned, Clark originally told the police that he left the party at 9:30 the next morning and everyone was safely asleep in the apartment. He claimed that whoever had assaulted the group had done it after he had left the premises.

But two young newspaper boys told a different version. They told the authorities that they both saw Clark near the Dillon home, wearing a bloodied shirt, around 4:30 a.m. or so, while they were delivering newspapers. He looked very disheveled.

The next morning, the fifteenth, Arthur Decker Brown wandered into the Rainbow Tavern on East Sprague Street, his face white. He was an employee at Dillon's sign shop and had knocked on the door and got no answer. The bartender asked him if he wanted a beer. Brown, in shock, said, "No, no. Go next door, around the back, see if you see what I saw. It's a massacre at the Dillons'…"

Worriedly, the bartender put down the glass he was cleaning and hurriedly made his way over to the Dillon house. He returned fairly quickly, face white, also in complete shock and immediately called the police.

When the investigators arrived at the horrible scene, they were horrified by what they saw. Blood was everywhere. They checked the pulse of all four victims. Mr. Dillon and the twenty-six-year-old Jane Staples were both stone cold. Mrs. Dillon had a very weak pulse, as did Mr. Winnett. They were rushed to the nearest hospital.

Police found the bloody hatchet used for the massacre just fifteen feet from the crime scene.

The police had several suspects to interview:

- Arthur Decker Brown: He had been fired from Dillon's sign shop just the day before the killings. He was also the first person to discover the victims.
- Edward Quentin: As Winnett was being rushed to the hospital, he kept repeating "Ed Quentin" over and over again. (Later, Quentin went to the police and cleared his name. It remains a mystery why Winnett was repeating his name.) Quentin was also an employee of Dillon's sign shop.
- Charles Staples: Jane's jealous husband, who knew for a fact that she was sleeping with three other men. Charles was said

to have a wicked temper, and the county prosecuting attorney announced that "Charles Staples is the coldest-blooded man I have ever met in all my years in the prosecuting office!" Others claimed Charles was also a Communist.

- Woodrow Clark: Who (after knowing he was caught) confessed to the killings.

Clark had blood on his shoes when arrested and questioned. Once he was in custody, his story changed again. He now told the police that Jane Staples was passed out in the bed next to him, and the Dillons were sleeping next to her. He claimed that he used the hatchet to chop wood for the stove so he could fry up bacon and eggs for breakfast. He left the Dillons' house at 2:30 a.m., after he cooked the meals. He said he then went back to his hotel room and didn't wake up until almost noon. His roommate noticed that Clark looked untidy. Clark told his roommate that he was lying in bed with one of the women, and Dillon came rushing into the bedroom with a gun. The two men began fighting, and Clark left the house at about 2:30 a.m.

AROUND LUNCHTIME LATER THAT day, Clark and his roommate decided to go get a beer at a nearby tavern. When they read the morning paper, they saw the articles regarding the murders. Clark found one of Dillon's business cards in his trousers, and he quickly tore it up and put it in an ashtray. (This was later collected as evidence and proved that Clark had been in contact with Mr. Dillon.) The newspaper announced that Mr. and Mrs. Dillon were both dead from an attack with an axe. Frank Stanish Winnett and Jane Staples were also both brutally attacked and rushed to the hospital. One only wonders what was going through Clark's mind that next morning, remembering the murders he committed in his drunken blur…

AT THE MORGUE, THE coroner determined that Mr. Dillon and Jane Staples had been killed sometime around five o'clock on the morning of the fifteenth. The undigested bacon and eggs in their stomachs revealed to the coroner that they had both eaten breakfast just a half hour or so before being killed. This contradicts Clark's story that he left the Dillons' home at 2:30 a.m., after he cooked breakfast. But being drunk, his time frames would probably be screwed up.

Meanwhile, at the hospital, Winnett was being treated for nine intense skull fractures caused by a sharp instrument or axe. He could not recall anything from the night (or morning) of the attack. He probably suffered a concussion, too.

Mrs. Flora Dillon was still in intensive care, struggling for her life. (She later died on the nineteenth.)

DURING THE PROSECUTION, IT was argued that Clark also attempted to rape Staples. Clark's defense attorneys told the jurors that this was a crime of passion and not premeditated, so it was not a capital offense. But in 1944, the combination of rape and murder would usually end with the death penalty. Although no real evidence of rape was obtained, Staples's panties did have bloody hand marks all over them, so it was assumed that Clark was trying to remove them to molest her while she was either unconscious or already dead. Did Mr. Dillon interrupt his attempts, which caused Clark to take the hatchet to him as well?

The jurors did not believe Clark's stories for a minute. And the nail in his coffin was when a pretty young girl walked into the room and Clark turned a "roving eye" at her and grinned. The jurors knew right then and there that Clark was a dangerous and ruthless criminal and probably was going to rape poor Jane.

Clark was finally sentenced to die on October 5, 1945, for first-degree murder charges. For unknown reasons, he was never tried for the murder and the attempted rape of his victim Jane Staples.

Clark was put in the execution chamber to wait for his sentence to play out. Oddly, just a few hours before he was to be executed, the governor called the warden and granted Clark a ninety-day stay. Why? He explained that they had received a large number of letters, petitions and phone calls begging for Clark to not be hanged, as most of the evidence was circumstantial. The petitioners completely ignored the fact that Clark had written and signed a confession to committing the murders. They demanded his sentence be changed to life imprisonment.

But they only prolonged his agony. Clark was again sentenced to hang, this time on February 4, 1946, almost two years after he brutally killed three people (four, if Winnett would have died).

On the fourth, guards and a chaplain remained at Clark's side until it was time. He was granted his last meal, which was a nice steak accompanied by a tall glass of cold milk (according to photographs).

In 1944, Woodrow Clark killed three people while partying in Spokane; he claimed he was so drunk he didn't remember taking the hatchet to them. *WSA/CD.*

At 11:30 p.m., Clark was read his death warrant and had to contemplate it for a while.

At 12:05 a.m., Clark was moved to the gallows, with his arms strapped closely to his sides. He was positioned over the trapdoor, and then they strapped his legs together firmly. A rope noose was tightened around his neck by an expert hangman, whose sole job was to conduct these procedures in a quick and painless manner.

Nearby, three volunteers all pressed the button they were assigned. (This way, no one would know for sure who pressed the actual button that would release the trapdoor.)

Clark's body struggled and bucked for a few minutes, then hung motionless.

Everyone waited exactly fifteen minutes, then a physician and a coroner both pronounced Clark officially dead.

Clark is buried at Mountain View Cemetery in Walla Walla, Washington. He was only twenty-nine years old. He was an ex-soldier, born in Kennebunk, Maine, and he worked at a shoe factory after he was discharged from the army in 1943. During the time of the murders, he was working as a dishwasher in a Spokane hotel.

Destiny and fate played cruel cards that drunken night in 1944.

If Clark had just not gone to the bar that night... If the Dillons had just gone home instead of buying more beer and inviting strangers into their home... If Clark had just gone back to his hotel room and slept off the liquor instead of drinking more... If Jane Staples had gone home to her husband (or boyfriend) instead of drinking herself unconscious and passing out in the bed of Mr. and Mrs. Dillon...

So many things could have gone differently that night, things that could have possibly saved the lives of three innocent victims. Or who knows; maybe not.

THE STRANGE HOMICIDE OF LISE ASPLUND

The first white man to be hanged from the gallows in Spokane (and the last person to be legally hanged by Spokane County) was George Webster (1871–1900).

Webster was known as a laborer and handyman, and he was considered hardworking and skilled by the locals. He had a hard life when he was young; both his parents died early, and he began to live on his own at the tender age of thirteen. He typically worked in the town of Cheney, near Spokane. In May 1897, Webster was twenty-six years old. One night, he was drinking in several saloons in Cheney until around seven o'clock, when Constable Brown politely asked Webster to leave town before he began causing any trouble. The drunken Webster decided to slowly make his way back home by walking toward Medical Lake. Soon tired, Webster decided to try to find a place to sleep it off for the night.

A family by the name of Asplund had a small farm near Cheney. Andrew Asplund was originally from Sweden; he immigrated to America in 1877 and married Lise Holm (1852–1897) in 1882. On this particular night, May 6, the inebriated Webster knocked on the door of the Asplund farm and asked if he could sleep there for the evening. The kind family took him in, not knowing that the evening's devastating events would change their lives forever.

Mr. Asplund desperately needed some help on the family farm, so the men made an arrangement that Webster could stay on and work for a few days for the decent wage of seventy-five cents per day plus board. Agreeing, the men shook on it. After dinner, the family soon went off to bed. The three men slept in the only bedroom in the house, and Lise and her two small girls (Ella May, age thirteen, and Jennie, age eleven) were all sleeping together in the kitchen.

During the night, Webster got thirsty and asked for some water. Asplund said, "There's a bucket of drinking water out on the porch." Webster stumbled his way through the kitchen and over toward the porch.

This is where things took a bad turn. Lise told the police officer later that Webster had "stopped and tried to touch her girls." Of course, the angry mother urgently shooed him out the door. Webster apparently got his water and then returned to bed. But soon, he decided he wanted some "medicine" (whiskey) and again left the bedroom.

Around 2.30 a.m., Lise again shooed him away, this time locking him out of the house. When Webster tried the door and found it locked, he became angry and demanded his coat and hat, as he was leaving and wanted to make his way onward to Medical Lake after all.

Lise, tired of the stranger, eagerly decided to give him his belongings so he could get on his way and out of their home for good. She put his hat and coat on the end of a broomstick and poked it out the kitchen window for him to retrieve. Lise thought she saw a second man outside with Webster, but the light was poor.

Soon the loud *bang, bang* of a gun being fired sounded through the air! The unsuspecting Lise was shot in the abdomen, the bullet lodging in her delicate spine. Her young girls watched in horror as their mother lay dying on the kitchen floor. Andrew immediately woke at the sound of the gunshots and ran to the kitchen with their son, John, age thirteen. As the family looked in shock at Lise bleeding at their feet, Webster wandered back into the house and asked who was shooting. Lise told her family that Webster was the one who shot her.

Strangely, Webster casually walked back into the bedroom and went to sleep.

Panicked, Andrew ran to his neighbor William Spence's house and asked for help. Spence's son George was ordered to go fetch a doctor and the police in the nearby town, Cheney.

In Cheney, Constable Abel Brown (the very same one who had ordered Webster to leave his town earlier that day), Town Marshal John Corbett and Dr. Francis Pomeroy were quickly dispatched and made their way back to the Asplund farm in their horse-drawn carriages.

It was around 5:00 a.m. when they finally arrived. Lise had gone back to bed in the kitchen, and oddly, Webster was still asleep in the bedroom as if nothing had happened.

When the marshal grabbed Webster to handcuff him, a .38-caliber revolver fell from his coat. He also had two pints of whiskey and several incriminating sex-oriented articles on him, all logged as evidence.

Lise identified Webster as the man who shot her before she was rushed off to the hospital in Medical Lake. Unfortunately, the bullet wound had gone untreated for so many hours that it was infected, and poor Lise had lost a good deal of blood.

Tragically, she died at 10:42 on Friday night.

ONCE THE WORD GOT out about Lise's death and the nightmare at the Asplund family farm, a large mob gathered at the jail and demanded Webster be lynched to death immediately. Constable Brown moved Webster to another prison to avoid something bad happening to his prisoner.

On May 10, Webster was charged with first-degree murder and sentenced to death by hanging. Webster pleaded not guilty on May 14, and the trial was set for September 15, 1897.

It was recorded in the *Spokane Daily Chronicle* that Webster told Lise in front of witnesses, "Yes, I shot you. I don't know why I did it. I am very sorry, and I hope you get well."

Complications with jurors and votes made the trial convoluted. Besides Lise's testimony prior to her death, no one else could say who had actually shot the gun. Was it Webster or the mysterious stranger lurking outside the farm at 2:30 a.m.? Many believed Webster shot Lise in anger because she locked him out of the house to protect her children from his drunken advances. And he *was* carrying a gun.

Webster was found guilty a second time, and the new execution date was scheduled for July 28, 1899 (after several years of appeals and ridiculous nonsense). He was to be hanged at the Spokane County Courthouse. But right before he was scheduled to be executed, an extension of life was granted by U.S. district judge Hanford.

For unknown reasons, six thousand people petitioned Governor Rogers for clemency but were refused. (Execution clemency is a plea for mercy from a convicted person for an act of grace or pardon.) Rogers held his ground, and the plea was never even considered. The people felt that life in prison was enough punishment for Webster, but his execution was put on the calendar anyway.

Two hundred people were invited to attend the execution. Ten days before the scheduled hanging, the scaffold and platform were unpacked, and they started to be assembled. The trapdoor had a fifty-pound weight attached to the underside of it.

Webster continued to claim, "I should not be convicted of a crime I do not remember committing because I was drunk!" The Asplund family and many other people felt he should hang for Lise's murder.

On the morning of his execution, Webster ate toast, eggs and coffee as his last meal at seven o'clock.

At nine o'clock, he was read his death sentence.

At eleven o'clock, he was led to the scaffold, where his final words were a simple, "Goodbye."

Webster is buried at the Greenwood Cemetery (now called Greenwood Memorial Terrace). Webster's execution cost Spokane County $896.90.

The Asplund family never truly recovered from the nightmare, and all of them ended up with severe mental issues that required institutionalization. It was a sad, tragic end for a family that was simply trying to help a stranger out.

SON SLAYS FATHER OVER TWENTY-FIVE DOLLARS FOR A NEW SUIT

The trial of the year began as soon as the teenage son of James "Jim" Sloane swung the axe that killed his father. Sidney, the seventeen-year-old boy, and his father were fighting one evening, when Sidney lost his temper. His dad had been drinking and was reportedly belittling his boy (as well as his wife). The rest of the affair that evening made headlines for years.

James Sloane was originally from New York and graduated from Yale University. While he and his family were living in California, he invested in a silver mine in the town of Mullan, Idaho. He wanted financial security for himself and his sons when they got older. The family then moved from San Francisco to Spokane. He soon became partners with a man known as Waldo Paine in a grocery store supply business, which they soon named the Sloane-Paine Company. He eagerly worked for the company, and the family lived in a nice home at 513 Sixth Avenue, on the corner of Sixth Avenue and Stevens Street.

Just one day before the gruesome murder, Sloane had taken Sidney into his office and proudly introduced him to his fellow workers. He took the boy from desk to desk, introducing his son to everyone with a big smile.

The next morning, when they read about their boss's brutal murder, his coworkers were all surprised and in complete shock.

Sloane's bloody body was discovered in the alley behind their family home by Mrs. James Petty, who lived next door at 501 Fifth Street, and she notified the police immediately. Mrs. Petty told her story to the officers:

I had risen at 3:45 a.m. in order to do the family washing before the heat of the day. A few minutes later, I noticed a man's foot in the alley, and next my attention was attracted by a young man motioning me to come downstairs. He told me that a drunken man was lying in the alley. When I went and checked, I found blood on the man's left hand and saw that he was dead. A wallet lay on his breast and papers from his pocket were strewn about the body.

The Spokane police quickly arrived at the alley to investigate the body of the dead man. They recognized him through the gashes and blood as Mr. Sloane.

The police officers walked over to the Sloane house, where they showed the Sidney boy the bloody towel that had been wrapped around his dead dad's head. Sidney began crying.

"Better shape up," said Sergeant McPhee.

"Where is he?" asked the boy, seemingly worried about his father.

McPhee motioned to the boy, then took him to the back alley where the corpse was still lying. Sidney dropped down next to his dad and became very emotional.

"Better find your mom," the officer said. Between grand sobs, Sidney told the cop that his mother was off camping out by Nine Mile Bridge with his brother. The officer felt an overwhelming sense of pity for the boy, kneeling next to the hacked-up corpse of his father. Until…

When the boy stood up, McPhee noticed that the boy had not really been crying. It was all for show. Not a single tear had really been shed. That was when McPhee *knew* he had his killer.

The coroner was called out to remove the body, while several other officers reviewed the crime scene. They found a bloody axe, a piece of a bloody carpet and bloody rags under the porch of the Sloane house. Inside, the keyholes were all stuffed with cotton, and the remaining carpet and walls told the gruesome tale of the last harrowing moments of the man's life. The bloody, smeared footprints of Mr. Sloane proved that he had obviously been trying to get away from his assailant. Spatters of blood, all on the high ceiling, suggested that the blows from the axe came down with great anger and strength.

THE BOY WAS ARRESTED by Detective McDermott, on orders from McPhee.

When the police tried to talk to the landlady of the Sloane home, she refused to comment.

Once caught, the boy tried to pin the crime on a man named Riley. When the police began questioning the boy about his dad's murder, he became silent. The officers had found fifty dollars in (blood-soaked) bills in the boy's pockets.

Just when the investigators thought Sidney would never talk, the officers mentioned his mother, and he broke down and said he wanted to talk.

He told the officers, "My dad had come home drunk, and we began arguing. I wanted to rob my dad of $500, I dunno why." Then he clammed up.

Chief Waller was running out of patience. "Sidney, I've lived near you a long time and I was a good friend to your father. Now I want you to tell me the true story about what happened."

Sidney looked up for the first time and quietly said, "Okay, I will."

Chief Waller relaxed and hoped the boy would finally come clean. "Who killed your father?"

Sidney Sloane's inmate card. He was deemed criminally insane after he killed his father over twenty-five dollars. *WSA.*

Without remorse or emotion, Sidney told the story:

I did it myself. We had words. Father came home and we talked for a while. Then he commenced to criticize me; said I was uneducated and unfit to do for myself and make a living. He said it was my mother's fault. And then he commenced to abuse her and said she was not respectable and cursed her. That angered me, for I have a violent temper. I went out to the neighbor's woodshed and got the ax. When I came back, I kept it behind my back. Father started the same talk again, and I killed him. Then I dragged the body downstairs, put it in a wheelbarrow and dumped it in the alley.

As his father's body was lying on a cold slab at the Buchanan Undertaking Company, Sidney was officially arrested for the murder. Since Sidney was not eighteen years of age, he would not be tried as an adult.

Dr. A.E. Pope, the man who performed the autopsy, revealed the results of his examination:

I found six wounds to the back of the head and on the face. The former cut through the scalp and fractured the bones of the skull. Food was found in the victim's mouth. The wounds that caused the death were one and a quarter inches long and three quarters of an inch wide, evidently made by a sharp instrument. The blows were delivered from behind the victim and while the head was bent forward.

89

Apparently, Mr. Sloane was eating dinner when Sidney decided to kill him. Spokane coroner Dr. F.P. Witter also disclosed his findings:

We found there was partially masticated food, bread and milk, in the mouth and that the man's stomach contained food that had barely been swallowed when the blows were struck. The man was unquestionably in the act of eating when he was slain. The position of the blows of the axe indicates that the gashes that cut through the man's skull were on the back of the head, indicating that he was bending over the table when the weapon fell. There was no struggle. The skull was badly fractured on each side, and the blows were so severe that they had cracked it lengthwise from the forehead to the base.

During the trial, a boarder in the Sloane home (who was upstairs in her room at the time of the murder) was brought to the witness stand. Mrs. Lily Syphers told the courtroom her version of what she witnessed:

On the night of the homicide, I was awakened, at what hour I cannot say exactly, by a noise of someone running in a light pair of shoes, running rapidly across the floor of the room occupied by the Sloanes. My mother's and my room is directly above it. Following this rushing noise came a sound of a heavy body falling. I fell back asleep and did not wake until the next morning about 5:30 a.m., when I was roused by the sound of someone using a hose outside my window.

Why did Lily not wake up her mom or go investigate the strange sounds?

Many witnesses testified that Mr. Sloane's memory was failing. The bookkeeper for Sloane-Paine during the time of the homicide, Herman Smith, was brought to the stand. He told the court, "In my briefings with Mr. Sloane, I found he would often speak gibberish, he was confused, he would ask me to dictate absolute nonsense, he would call me by the wrong name, he would overdraw the accounts and was generally drunk most of the time."

When Smith was asked about his dealings with the young Sidney, he said, "I thought Sidney was for sure insane. He would tell me wild stories: that he was engaged to thirty-two different ladies, of his bizarre money-making schemes and that he was going to raise expensive goats in Wyoming. One time he went into a craze and broke into the wine cellar, busted the top off a bottle of wine and proceeded to drink it straight from the broken bottle."

A rare photograph of Spokane's ruthless legal prosecutor Fred Pugh. *The* Spokane Press, *May 1, 1909.*

More witnesses spoke of Sidney's strange actions, from stealing items from the office to becoming wildly enraged during an innocent game of pool. One of the most damaging allegations against Sidney came from the family's former cook, a Chinese man named H.D. Lee. He took to the stand and told a very disturbing story about Sidney: "One time, Sidney got an axe and chased his smaller brother around the house, talking and screaming irrationally."

Deputy Prosecuting Attorney Fred Pugh told the jury their options for sentencing. "If he is convicted of murder in the first degree, he will be hanged. Murder in the second degree will be ten years to life in prison. Manslaughter would get him a sentence of one to twenty years." He wanted to make sure the jurors knew the consequences of their sentence for Sidney.

AFTER A VERY EXPENSIVE, forty-two-day-long trial, the jurors finally came to their decision. Attorney Robertson announced, "Sidney Sloane is found not guilty of the murder of Mr. James Sloane due to temporary insanity. Both his mother and myself agree that he shall be kept in custody until his sanity is proven, locked up for life if necessary."

As Sidney was being led from the courtroom back to the jail, he sneered at Sheriff Doak and said, "Well, we stuck it into you, didn't we?" and laughed.

Sheriff Doak was not amused: "Shut up, you little whelp."

The next item the court would have to agree on was whether Sidney was to be committed to an insane asylum or admitted to the state penitentiary. It was decided Sidney would go to the Walla Walla State Penitentiary. Warden Kincaid would transfer the boy himself. The boy dressed in a fine black suit— a suit that some suggest was the very reason the boy lost his temper that fateful night of the killing. Sidney had desired a new suit and went to the tailor the very day before he butchered his dad. The tailor needed a twenty-five-dollar deposit in order to sew the custom suit. That evening, Sidney asked Mr. Sloane for the money. His dad refused. Sidney lost his temper, and the rest is history.

Ironically, for the trial, his mother paid the tailor the money required to make the suit so Sidney would have a nice one to wear.

Now, as Sidney rode the train, with Sheriff Doak sitting by his side, he was again wearing the very same suit. When they stopped at a diner on the way to the prison, Sidney had a ferocious appetite and ordered oysters as well as just about everything else on the menu. Doak only picked at his food. He was disgusted by Sidney.

Sidney Sloane became inmate #4351 at the Walla Walla State Penitentiary on December 27, 1906. He was then eighteen years old and listed as "criminally insane." Attorney Roberts announced, "I will not be doing habeas corpus proceedings to try to free Sidney. I do not want him freed. And he is to be treated as an insane person, not a criminal."

Records indicate that Attorney Robertson and Ida Huff, Sidney's mother, were trying to get Sidney released just a few years later. He was finally released from Walla Walla prison on January 16, 1929.

Sidney went on to live a nice long life. He later got married, at age sixty, to Ruth King, and they lived a quiet life as farmers in the Nine Mile area in Spokane. When Sidney was seventy-eight, he was admitted to St. Luke's Hospital in Spokane, where, after thirteen long days, he eventually succumbed to acute congestive heart failure and died.

No autopsy was performed.

CHAPTER 5
WASHINGTON'S PRISONS

Walla Walla State Penitentiary

Walla Walla State Penitentiary was built in 1886 (before Washington was even a state), and the prison was originally called the Washington Territorial Prison. Lawmakers allowed $96,000 toward the construction of the territory's first extensive prison. In the very first year, ninety-seven men were trapped behind its bars.

The prison could eventually hold up to 2,200 inmates. Prisoners used to call it the "Walls." If an inmate ended up at Walla Walla, they were typically doomed, for that was where prisoners were sent if they were on death row (sentenced to be executed). When Washington became an official state in 1889, the prison's name changed to the Washington State Penitentiary.

The prison cells were constructed of solid steel—the walls, the floors and the ceilings—to prevent the possibility of escape. Men were housed two per cell.

One of the youngest-ever inmates was a boy just twelve years of age named Herbert Niccolls Jr. (1919–1983). Herbert grew up in a very troubled family that suffered from extreme poverty. He was sent to school in dirty, ragged clothes and without any shoes. When he was just nine years old, his father shot and killed a neighbor, mistaking her for Herbert's mother. Mr. Niccolls was promptly sent to an insane asylum. Herbert's mother could not properly care for her nine children, so she gave the boys away and kept

Armed Walla Walla State Penitentiary guards stand on the tower landings, watching over the inmates below. *WSA.*

the girls. Herbert ended up in multiple foster homes, being bounced from home to home. He stole from his foster parents and caused trouble, so he ended up in a juvenile facility. When he was released, he went to live with his grandma, Mary Addington, who had no interest in providing a loving home for young Herbert. Instead, she starved him half to death and brutally beat him regularly, insisting he was "possessed by demons."

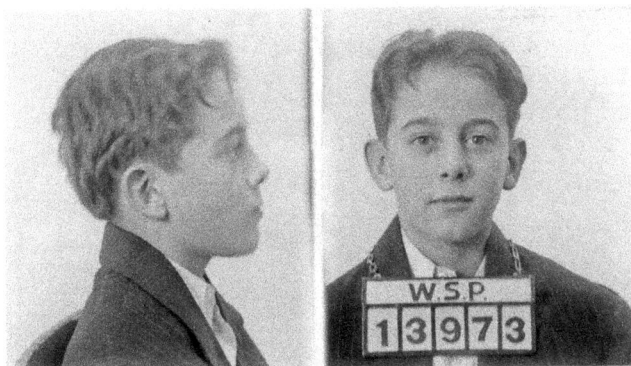

Herbert Niccolls was only twelve years old when he was sentenced to life in prison at the Washington State Penitentiary for killing a policeman. *WSA/CD.*

After suffering years of this abuse, he ran away and set out on his own with nothing more than the tattered clothes on his back and a stolen .32-caliber Iver-Johnson pistol. On August 5, 1931, the starving boy went about trying to rob Peter Klaus's People's Supply Store in Asotin, Washington, of candy and tobacco. When the sheriff was called by the owner, the police soon showed up to see what was going on.

"Come on out, boy," called seventy-three-year-old Sheriff John Leonard Wormell. When he heard no response, he slowly entered the store. The frightened boy jumped out from behind a barrel and shot the sheriff right in the head. Wormell died instantly. The boy was taken to Asotin County jail.

The deputy involved, Wayne Bezona, was concerned about the boy's safety and had him transferred to Garfield County Jail. At his trial, Herbert was found guilty and sentenced to life in prison. He was sent to Washington State Penitentiary with a dreaded life sentence hanging over his head.

But young Herbert flourished within the boundaries of jail. It was the first time in his entire life so far that he was getting food regularly, not being abused, following a schedule, receiving medical attention and feeling like people cared about him.

The warden and other officers liked Herbert and took good care of the boy. They even helped him learn to read. Worried about sexual predators, they had him sleep in a separate little hut (away from the other prisoners) that was situated near the guards, to keep him safe. In the ten years Herbert was in jail, he was allowed to learn various school subjects, and in 1938, he proudly received his high school diploma. Herbert had a knack for math and later signed up for classes provided by Washington State College. He was pardoned in 1941 at age twenty-one and was released into the real world to start his new life.

Prisoners, dressed in their striped uniforms, are confined inside the Walla Walla State Penitentiary. *WSA.*

Herbert moved to California, near Hollywood, where he got a good job as an accountant for MGM; he later was employed by 20th Century Fox. He married, had a son and lived a quiet, productive life. Herbert made a good and honest living after he was released from Washington State Penitentiary. In 1983, he suffered a heart attack and died at age sixty-four.

If Herbert had been provided a safe, loving and secure home life when he was a child, he might have succeeded in school and never gotten in trouble at all. He probably would never have shot a man and ended up in jail for life.

Herbert became a model citizen, and he definitely did not have "demons" in him.

ON THE OTHER SIDE of the coin, one of the most horrible killers confined in Washington State Penitentiary was Jack Owen Spillman, called the Werewolf Butcher from Spokane. In 1995, Spillman ruthlessly killed three people and bragged to everyone who would listen that he wanted to become the "most famous serial killer." Luckily, he was captured before he carried out his threat.

Years later, the prison was considered "inhuman" by the media, and a frenzy of riots started. Thus, it began to get a remodel and multiple upgrades.

The Washington State Penitentiary is still in operation today and is situated on 540 acres near Walla Walla, Washington. It can house between 1,968 and 2,500 criminals.

McNeil Island Corrections Center

When it closed in 2011, McNeil Island Corrections Center was the oldest prison in the Northwest, and it has an interesting history. The following information is from the Washington State Department of Corrections website.

- 1873: The original cell house was built on McNeil Island.
- 1875: A jail was opened as the first federal prison in Washington Territory and consumed almost twenty-eight acres of beautiful waterside land. It had only nine prisoners.
- 1889: The first warden was Gilbert Palmer, and he had the help of seven guards.
- 1904: McNeil was declared an official United States prison.
- 1927: An additional twenty-seven acres was purchased for a garden.
- 1931: An additional 1,618 acres was purchased for a water supply.
- 1947: The prison held 320 inmates.
- 1948: A community center and school was built for the children of the island.

Seven unidentified guards at McNeil Island Federal Penitentiary pose with their weapons. *WSA.*

- 1976: The facility was declared obsolete.
- 1981: The last four inmates were shipped off the island.
- 1984: The seven-square-mile island was deeded to the state from the federal government, and it became part of a protected wildlife reserve.
- 1989: The facility received $90 million for upgrades and improvements.
- 1990: The facility was awarded $392 million for upgrades and improvements.
- 1993: Five new buildings were erected, each with the capacity to hold 256 inmates. A sixth building was also added, so now the prison could hold 1,300 inmates. The balance of the island, 3,119 acres, was deeded to the Washington State Department of Fish & Wildlife.
- 2011: McNeil Island Corrections Center was officially closed after 136 years housing dangerous prisoners.

From 1961 to 1966, Charles Manson was locked up in McNeil. Two years after his release, his cult crew killed pregnant Sharon Tate and several others. *California Department of Corrections, public domain.*

In 1961, Charles Manson (1934–2017) was transferred to McNeil Island Corrections Center, where he remained until 1966. Three years later, his cult members killed Sharon Tate, her unborn child and several others. Manson remained in jail for the rest of his life. He died from cardiac arrest resulting from respiratory failure and colon cancer at the hospital on November 19, 2017. It had cost California taxpayers almost $2 million to house, feed and provide medical care for Manson. He had been found guilty of multiple murders.

ROBERT "BIRDMAN OF ALCATRAZ" Stroud (1890–1963) was one of the more famous inmates who spent time on McNeil Island. Stroud was born in Seattle, Washington, under the influence of an abusive father. He stopped going to school in the third grade. He ran away from home at age thirteen, and when he was eighteen, he ended up working as a pimp in Alaska. In 1909, when a bartender named F.K. von Dahmer was violent toward Stroud's mistress/prostitute, Kitty O'Brien, Stroud shot and killed him. Stroud was sent to McNeil Island Corrections Center for twelve years and was a very difficult prisoner. His bad behavior landed him an additional six months in jail. In 1912, he was sent to Leavenworth prison in Kansas. There he stabbed and killed a guard named Andrew Turner in the mess hall. He was again sentenced to death, but President Woodrow Wilson changed his sentence to life in prison instead. It was in the Kansas prison that the "birdman" developed his keen interest in birds. How? A tiny bird had fallen into the prison yard, and he nursed it back to health. For some reason, he

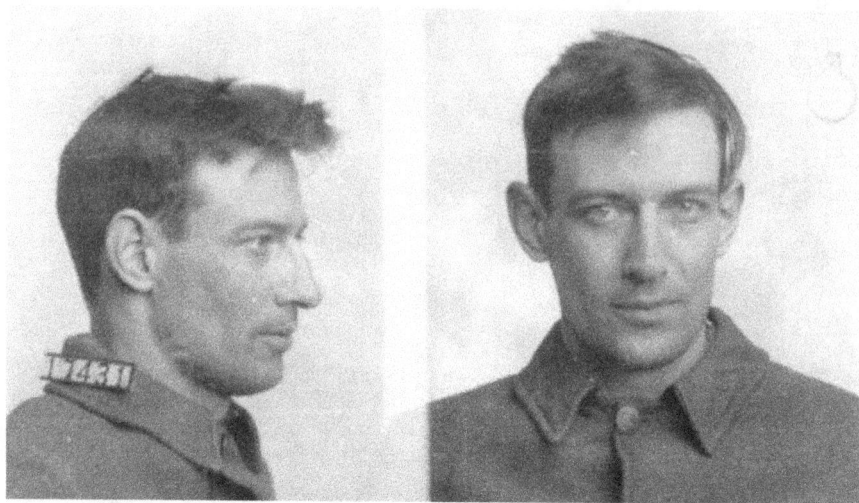

The notoriously violent inmate Robert "Birdman of Alcatraz" Stroud spent the years 1909–12 in McNeil prison. *United States federal government, public domain.*

was allowed to raise and breed canaries, to the extent that he housed over three hundred birds in tiny cigar boxes in a neighboring cell. He wrote two books and became an avid ornithologist.

But Stroud's life in jail took a turn for the worse when he was transferred (without his birds) to Alcatraz in 1942. He died in his cell on November 21, 1963.

THE MAN WHO ESCAPED TWO FEDERAL PRISONS AND ONE GOVERNMENT JAIL

One of the most interesting convicts to be housed in McNeil Island Corrections Center was a man named Walter E. Layman, originally from Tacoma, Washington. His criminal life started pretty early. In 1907, at the age of sixteen, he became part of a group of men who roamed the streets of Spokane. They would commit petty crimes: small robberies, pickpocketing, gambling.

One day, the gang sent out their newest member to go begging in the streets. When he returned with a bag of coins, they demanded he share his loot with them. The boy refused. The gang brutally beat the boy, so badly that he ended up dying. The ruthless gang could not have cared less. They took his money and threw his body into the Spokane River.

Layman and six others were arrested, but no one was ever convicted for the boy's murder.

In 1911, Layman was arrested for counterfeiting over $2,000 worth of bank notes in Seattle. This earned him three years in jail at McNeil Island. In July 1912, Layman managed to escape while working on an excavation for the prison. It took over an hour for the guards to finally discover he was missing from the group. Once his absence was noticed, the warden put out an immediate call for an extensive search of the island. Over one hundred men were hired to look for Layman; they were paid four dollars per eight-hour shift and were also offered a fifty-dollar reward to boot. About fifty boats surrounded the island, with men eagerly looking out for Layman trying to escape off the island. They knew he could not swim, but that didn't mean a pal would not come to the island in a boat and rescue him.

For three days, Layman was able to hide from the search parties, but after days of eating only wild berries to survive, he approached a local farmer named Oscar Anderson for food. Anderson, eager for the reward, gave notice to the authorities that Layman was at his ranch. He was captured at ten o'clock in the morning on July 20, just two and a half miles from the prison, looking thin and tired.

LAYMAN WAS LATER MOVED (along with thirteen other men) to Leavenworth prison in Kansas in September of 1912, to relieve the overcrowding McNeil Island was experiencing.

Layman settled into Leavenworth prison and was housed with a man named Osborne. The two soon began fantasizing about escaping the jail—and they somehow succeeded.

The daring escape was brainstormed by Layman himself and his thirty-six-year-old cellmate, Richard L. Osborne (inmate #6542). Osborne, originally from Texas, had been sentenced to eighteen years for a robbery he committed in Washington, D.C. He had made three previous attempts at escaping the prison. The two made a great pair; Layman had already escaped from prison once, while he was serving time in a government prison on the Pacific Coast. Osborne was the prison shoemaker; he was well liked and had a great sense of humor. People were naturally drawn to him, and the guards enjoyed his company.

In the summer of 1913, the men finally perfected their escape plan. They managed to saw through both their cell door bars and the nearby window bars. They devised a makeshift seat with hooks to pull themselves up and out of the window. They secured a getaway ride from friends who were waiting outside. They made dummies of themselves that lay "sleeping soundly" in their cots, so the two men's absence from their cots would not alarm the guards.

The whole escape went as planned. No one even knew they were gone. Until one of the guards discovered the sawed bars…

Around midnight, the guards had thought they heard a motorcar just outside the prison, but they did not bother to investigate. After the men's escape, the guards found their wooden plank seat outside, near the road.

The warden at the time, R.W. McClaughry, told the press, "It was one of the most daring escapes I remember since I've been in prison work, thirty-nine years. Osborne ranks with Dick Turpin and other dangerous men in prison history."

A nationwide search began for the convicts.

Later, a mysterious package showed up at the ranch of the farmer who turned Layman in to the police. The package appeared to be a book titled *Where Half the World Is Waking Up*, by Clarence Poe. Suspicious, Oscar Anderson threw the package in a tub of water. Sure enough, the "book" was actually a homemade bomb! The interior pages had been cut out and the empty space filled with emery paper, matches, dynamite caps and gunpowder. Was this payback to Anderson for turning Layman in to the police? Most likely.

LATER, LAYMAN WAS FOUND and shot by Spokane fire captain Fred Grant while he was walking down Washington Street. The bullet paralyzed Layman, and he was rushed to the hospital. Federal officers swarmed to arrest Layman the minute he could be moved, but death took the criminal before the lawmen took Layman back to jail.

PART II
MAYHEM

I hear you say, "How unlucky I am that this should happen to me." But not at all. Perhaps, say how lucky I am that I am not broken by what has happened, and I am not afraid of what is about to happen. For the same blow might have stricken anyone, but not many would have absorbed it without capitulation and complaint.

— *Marcus Aurelius,* Meditations

CHAPTER 1
POLICE CORRUPTION AND A DEAD BABY

D uring the first decade of 1900, the police department of Spokane was considered the most corrupt system in the United States. Although there were many great and honorable police officers on the force, many officers knew of and participated in illegal gambling, illegal prostitution and illegal drinking. All in a day's work!

ONE OF THE MOST sensationalized and multifaceted examples of this corruption was in 1910, in what came to be known as the Elliott-Gilder case. The level of immorality, bribery, tampering with evidence and dishonesty was both shocking and revolting. To relay the entire sordid story in one chapter would be ridiculous, as the scenario went on (or so it seemed to the citizens of Spokane) for decades.

The case became so entangled with so many different avenues of deceit that it is seriously hard to follow. And one single ghastly aspect of the whole affair is extremely hard to process.

WHAT BEGAN AS AN illegal affair with a minor by a Spokane police officer quickly escalated to a nationwide media sensation. Many careers, marriages and lives were ruined. An overwhelming number of details about the police force emerged daily, until the citizens of Spokane were up in arms and demanded dozens of people be thrown in jail.

During the sensational Spokane Police Department scandal in 1910, Officer Gilder was in trouble for impregnating Rose Elliott. The police department was also accused of letting the female prostitutes conduct their "business" from the jail cells. *LOC.*

Journalists were having a ball with the frenzy, until they started getting threats and ransom demands.

Spokane police officer L.D. Gilder began having sex with a young girl named Rose Elliott. To make matters worse, Rose became pregnant. To make matters even worse, she had a late-term abortion, and the baby's body was burned in a cookstove.

Police chief John T. Sullivan stood up for Gilder at all costs—until it cost him his job. Sullivan was getting pressured to remove Gilder from the force, and if he wasn't going to do it, then it was demanded that the mayor step in and fire Gilder. But Sullivan was in his own world of trouble. He had attempted to stop the exposure of a conspiracy to arrest a local editor, who was framed. He also repeatedly allowed houses of ill fame to operate (they were closed occasionally only to protect the police department). It was stated that more houses of prostitution were opened and allowed to run under Sullivan and Mayor Pratt than ever before.

Sullivan used a local prostitute named Sadie Evahn as a stool pigeon to tarnish the reputation of Mr. Smyth, a man of the press. Sadie pounced on Smyth and seduced him on Sullivan's orders. It was later suggested that he was part of a conspiracy, participating with a "certain lewd woman" named Sadie, and she, in turn, threatened to go to the press with all her information if he didn't play by Sullivan's rules. She allegedly set up a "matter of business" spot in room forty-four in the Congress Hotel in Spokane just for these sexual setups planned by Sullivan.

Rumor had it that, on one occasion, sixty girls were put in jail for sex trafficking, and their attorneys were not allowed to see or represent them. Strangely, the notorious Black prostitute who called herself Marie Taylor was allowed to continue to run her lodging house over the Minneapolis Bar, even while she was stuck in jail. Sullivan turned a blind eye to Taylor's actions, as well.

OFFICER GILDER ALWAYS SEEMED to be a few steps ahead of the law. Whenever prosecutors Logan and Doak got a lead about Gilder's location, they found out that Gilder had just left, warning the witnesses to flee or to withhold information.

On the last day of April, an elusive witness named Mrs. Gladys Britton, who lived in the same building as Rose, was found and captured by "Blondie Wood" Constable out of Justice Hyde, a few miles out of Spokane. Britton was being hidden at the house of Mrs. Young (the landlady of the lodging house).

But the month of May would be a harrowing one for all involved.

The most horrible and devilish thing imaginable happened.

Rose Elliott was pregnant with Officer Gilder's unwanted baby. A midwife named Mary Kelsch was hired to perform an illegal abortion. Gilder was to pay twenty-five dollars for the procedure, but he did not have enough money, so he borrowed it from Mrs. Pearce. (He only made two payments of $7.50 and $9.00; he never paid back the final balance of $6.50!) Pearce later admitted she was protecting Gilder from being accused of a crime.

What happened to the baby after the abortion is unthinkable.

A witness at the trial, Mrs. Gladys Britton, told the details of what happened that horrible night. "I live at East 115½ Sprague Avenue. I saw the body of a child wrapped in a towel and resting in a chair. It had a blood clot or hole in its head. Later I was told that Mrs. Kelsch had burned the baby in the cookstove." Britton wanted to then flee the country as well, but her husband, a fireman for the railroad, demanded she return to the station and tell the whole truth.

"As I said, I do not know positively what they had done to the child's body, but I believe that it had been burned in the cookstove as first announced in Mrs. Rigg's statement." Gladys lowered her eyes at what she was about to tell the inspector next. "I detected an *odor* coming from the cookstove, on which breakfast was currently being prepared. When I moved to the stove to poke the fire, I was strictly warned by Mrs. Pearce to leave it alone!"

On May 3, a witness, Mrs. Patie Riggs of 210 East First Avenue, signed an affidavit and went to the press to relay her story: "I know who committed the abortion." She implicated Nellie Pearce, Gladys Britton and Mary Kelsch in the matter. Pugh was immediately sent to investigate the women. On May 6, he questioned Britton and Pearce. Both women denied having any knowledge of the abortion. But the very next morning, the women packed their belongings and desired to flee Spokane and head to Canada. But Pugh was no dummy; he instantly issued warrants for their arrests. That same day, Doak and Logan went to the lodging house on East Sprague, hoping to find Pearce and Britton; they found that the two were long gone. Doak and Logan discovered that Gilder had gotten to Pearce and Britton first and told them to leave as soon as possible. Gilder recommended that they flee to British Columbia.

Surprisingly, probably weary of it all, Pearce showed up at the prosecuting attorney's office and surrendered herself. She exposed Gilder's efforts to suggest that she and Britton leave the country. What Pearce told Pugh remained in his memory forever.

She told him, "The Elliott girl had a baby that we delivered in one of the rooms at East Sprague Avenue. I deny any knowledge of the baby being burned in the cookstove. I thought the baby was buried over by the Northern Pacific railroad tracks. The abortion was performed by a woman that has not been arrested yet [meaning Mrs. Riggs]."

Deputy Sheriff Walter Logan and Coroner Schlegal promptly asked Pearce to take them to the spot where the baby was supposedly buried.

On May 9, an official police commissioner's investigation into the case began. The police commissioner also put a reward out for Mrs. Kelsch's capture.

After much intimidation in May, Gilder finally confessed to Prosecuting Attorney Pugh about his illicit affair with the underage girl, Rose Elliott.

He even confessed that he was having sex with her while she was being kept in a room (for her protection) that he and fellow officer H.W. Hood had rented for her on East Sprague Avenue for two weeks. (It is unclear if Rose was also having sex with Hood; she did seem to have a keen interest in and appetite for men in uniform.) When Rose's father, J.H. Elliott (an ex-soldier), found out she was being held in a room by the officers, he grew angry and attacked several officers, and his actions landed him in jail as well. Then the whole matter became twisted, and it was rumored that Gilder and Hood arrested Elliott to get him out of the way, so Gilder could continue his illicit affair with Rose.

Chief Sullivan was getting pressure from every angle to arrest Gilder. He announced, "All are lies."

Gilder was finally arrested at 5:10 p.m. on May 9 by Pugh, for tampering with state evidence. His sentence would be a $1,000 fine and a year in jail. He eagerly sued the press for $20,000 for defamation of his so-called character.

The Peyton Building at 700 Block West Sprague Avenue, on the northeast corner of Sprague and Post, in 1902, with Jacob Stusser, Pacific Loan, the Bank Saloon, J. Anderson & Co., Fine Liquors, Key West Cigars and a piano store. *The Dwight Collection, SPL/NWR.*

Above: The Higby building, later known as the Grand Hotel, on the northwest corner of Main and Howard, around 1900. *The Teakle Collection, SPL/NWR.*

Opposite: The Spokane Hotel, where Rose Elliott lounged after her sensational trial. This building was only two stories high at the time of the 1889 fire. *SPL/NWR.*

Later, Gilder was said to yell out at anyone who would listen, "If I am to go to Walla Walla State Penitentiary in connection with the more serious phases of the Elliott case, I will tell enough to send half of the police force to prison!" And everyone knew he would keep his promise. He did confess to Pugh that he was having sexual relations with Rose Elliott while he and Hood had her held in the room at the hotel. Hood told Pugh that they were holding her in the room because she had the mumps.

According to the testimony of James Wilson, a local painter, there was continuous illegal gambling going on at the back of the Havana Cigar Store on Sprague Avenue. The proprietors were suspicious: Tom Dickey and Denny Sullivan. Was Denny Sullivan related to Chief John Sullivan? Possibly, as poker games were allowed to run all night at that location, and a certain amount of money was silently kicked back to the city. This local illegal gambling was being allowed to carry on without any arrests by

Officer Sullivan, which only made his character less credible to the citizens of Spokane.

For her safety, Rose Elliott was placed under the protection and watchful eyes of the women running the Home of Good Shepherd convent. She told the women, "I am going to Oregon to get married." They calmly told her that she could not, as she was the star witness in two Superior Court cases against Mrs. Pearce and Mrs. Kelsch.

But Rose Elliott had other plans. She coerced two teenage boys into helping her escape. She tied bedsheets together and lowered herself down from her dorm room to the gardens below. She casually stayed the night in the Grand Hotel, and the next night she stayed at the Spokane Hotel. A few weeks later, it was reported by Mr. Bowman, proprietor of a grocery store on the corner of Fiske and Fifth in Union Park, that he overheard Sullivan speaking with Rose on the phone. Was Sullivan in on her escape so she could not be a star witness in the trial?

SULLIVAN FINALLY RESIGNED FROM office. He had now been in jail for several months. Mayor Pratt appointed a new chief—the ex-sheriff of Spokane, W.J. Doust—to the position. Rose was quickly found and unwillingly coerced back into the exhausting trials. Then she quickly changed her story again and said that she was afraid of her foster father. She claimed that *he* was the father of her first baby when she became pregnant in 1903—much to the horror of Mrs. Helen Elliott. Helen stood up and quickly told the court that the elderly Elliott could never have gotten Rose pregnant, because he had been involved in a bad horse accident years before Rose got pregnant and had been impotent ever since.

Then Helen tearfully told the court the other problems Rose had caused the family after they adopted her. "We adopted Rosie in Glencoe, Minneapolis, when she was already pregnant with a child. The little baby, also named Helen, was born. She is now seven years old. Our family moved to Spokane in 1903. When Mr. Elliott demanded to know *who* had gotten her pregnant, Rose blurted out, 'Your brother Ernie, in Minneapolis!'" The stunned foster parents did not know what to think. When Ernie was confronted about the scenario, he quickly made a trip to Spokane to straighten things out.

Helen continued, "Before Ernie arrived, Rose had come to me and said, 'My God, Mama, what will I do? I have told a lie of Ernie; he is not the father of my child!'" Apparently, Rose had been sleeping with many men and had no idea who the father of the baby was.

Outside the gates of the courthouse, Sullivan shook his head. He quietly said to Police Commissioner Tuerke, "She's a bad one [Rose]. She's a bad one. All you can do to those boys [Sullivan and Hood] is reprimand them."

THINGS SEEMED TO SETTLE down at the close of 1909, until elderly Elliott decided to make an uninvited visit to the house where Rose was working. He came straight through the door with a revolver and made advances toward Rose. He said he was wild with desire. Had Rose been telling the truth about

The spectacular Spokane County Courthouse in 1900, where many criminals met their final fate. *WSA.*

Mr. Elliott making advances toward her, after all? He was quickly arrested and just as quickly released with a warning. He promptly marched back to 1702 Monroe Street and went after Rose again. Officer Gilder stepped in this time and hauled the old man off to jail. Mrs. Helen Elliott was heartbroken over the confusing incident.

The trials seemed to lose their spark, and life more or less returned to normal—for some people.

The sketchy man named Sullivan was not one of them.

In late November, Sullivan shot a boy named Joe Curry and then tried to bribe his mother with fifty dollars to forget about the incident. It was soon discovered that Sullivan's real name was Lee Downey. He was quickly implicated in six other charges, along with Hogan. Sullivan/Downey quit the police force and strategically fled to Honduras, the only country at that time that did not have an extradition treaty with the United States.

It's hard to imagine that one young girl could cause so much chaos in so many people's lives.

CHAPTER 2

THE IWW AND THE BANNING OF FREE SPEECH

I f the Spokane Police Department wasn't already encountering enough bad press and complications, the year 1909 brought more by the wagonload daily.

The 1909 free speech fight in Spokane became the most important battle to protect free speech in the history of the United States.

The oppression of free speech in the city took a tragic turn for the worse. Citizens and workers had been pushed to their limits. During a time when there were hundreds of men out of work, over twenty employment agencies sprang up in Spokane. The problem was that these agencies were actually taking advantage of the men. They would charge each man one dollar to get a job; then the men would be fired after just a day or two of work, thus becoming unemployed again, so they would have to return to the agency and pay *another* dollar…

This vicious cycle became a complete racket and shame to the city. Workers were fed up and furious. They began demanding their rights to work gainfully. They would preach and yell about their troubles to anyone who would listen. Hundreds of men would stand on top of crates and tell the world how unfairly they were being treated.

On January 18, 1909, more than a few men had lost their patience with the employment agencies. A mob stormed into the Red Cross Employment Agency on Stevens Street and began destroying the furniture. The frightened agency workers were in shock. A fight started when a man demanded a refund of his one dollar and was refused. Angry, the

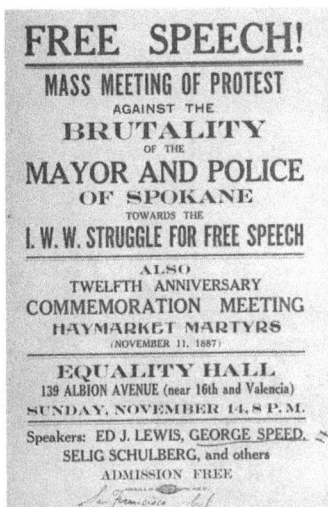

FREE SPEECH!

MASS MEETING OF PROTEST
AGAINST THE
BRUTALITY
OF THE
MAYOR AND POLICE
OF SPOKANE
TOWARDS THE
I. W. W. STRUGGLE FOR FREE SPEECH

ALSO
TWELFTH ANNIVERSARY
COMMEMORATION MEETING
HAYMARKET MARTYRS
(NOVEMBER 11, 1887)

EQUALITY HALL
139 ALBION AVENUE (near 16th and Valencia)
SUNDAY, NOVEMBER 14, 8 P.M.

Speakers: ED J. LEWIS, GEORGE SPEED,
SELIG SCHULBERG, and others
ADMISSION FREE

A free-speech poster announcing a protest against the Spokane police and the city's mayor, organized by the IWW workers' union. *WSA.*

men attacked Jack Hastings and beat him up; they also knocked a few teeth loose. Lumberjacks William Roberts and Rudolf Ling were among the men arrested for disorderly conduct. The other men ran back into the streets. The working men of Spokane were fed up.

The City Council finally took action—but not a very good one. On January 1, 1909, they implemented an ordinance that prohibited public speaking (except for a few chosen organizations and people, of course!). This infuriated the people of Spokane even more. Pretty soon, the police were arresting men and throwing them in jail for speaking in public. The jails became overcrowded very quickly. The situation became so intense that it caught the attention of an organization called the Industrial Workers of the World (IWW). An IWW organizer named James Walsh and other IWW members quickly came to Spokane to try to help out their fellow men. Walsh printed in the *Industrial Worker* newsletter and told everyone he saw, "Come and help fill the jail in Spokane!"

Soon, hundreds of fellow IWW members were coming to the city to help protest.

But no sooner than a man stood up on his soapbox on Stevens Street and the words "Fellow workers…" came out of his mouth, the officers yanked him down by the arm and handcuffed him. The next man would get up on the box, and he, too, would be yanked down and arrested. On November 2, 103 men in all were arrested, beaten and jailed. Over the next thirty days, over 500 men were put in jail.

A young married woman named Elizabeth Gurley Flynn (1890–1964) decided that she wanted to help the men of Spokane. Her father, Thomas Flynn (1854–1943), was a head organizer for the IWW. She came to Spokane when she was just sixteen years old (and pregnant with her second child), intent on making a difference in the free speech fight.

When she arrived, she showed up on Stevens Street, where all the commotion was happening, to try her hand at the soapbox. Much to the officers' surprise, she also chained herself to a nearby lamppost.

Above: Stevens Street is where many protested for their right to free speech, among the piles of horse manure. The Mohawk Block building is on the left. *WSA*.

Left: The strong Elizabeth Flynn wanted to help the IWW protesters, so she chained herself to a lamppost but was hauled off to jail anyway. *LOC*.

Flynn yelled from her crate at the top of her lungs, "This fight is serious! It *must* be won! Remember, an injury to one is an injury to us all! We must never give up! We have just begun the fight!"

The frustrated police eventually were able to break the chain and promptly dragged the young woman off to jail.

Flynn was thrown in a cell with two other women, both of whom were there on charges of prostitution. In her jail cell, Flynn was disgusted by the way the prisoners were treated. They were given dirty, lice-infested blankets for warmth and served gross stews and bad coffee.

But the horror she observed was only just getting started. Flynn noticed that the jailors would come grab the two women at all hours of the night and take them somewhere. They would be gone for some time, only to return, then be removed again a few moments later. It came out that the police officers and the jailors were allowing these women to continue to conduct their prostitution business—and the downstairs rooms were being used as an in-house brothel!

Flynn also learned that the only reason they did not attempt to abuse her was that they discovered she was in a "delicate" condition, and they did not trust her. One man did attempt to touch her, and when Flynn was awakened by him, she demanded, "Take your hands off me! I did not come here to be insulted!"

Although Flynn was arrested another ten times in the course of her stay in Spokane, she did manage to make a big difference for the free speech cause.

She also caused a lot of unwanted trouble and problems for the police department. After her first release from jail, she exposed the inside prostitution ring of the female prisoners in the next issue of the *Industrial Workers* newsletter. She reported on the horrible, filthy conditions of her cell and told the complete story of what she saw. She also collected sworn affidavits from other female prisoners about how they had been treated by the police; they were so horrible they could not even be printed in the paper.

As soon as the newsletter was printed and distributed, and Chief of Police Sullivan got wind of what it contained, officers were instructed to go door to door and confiscate and destroy all of the copies they could find.

The Spokane Police Department had enough on its plate; it did not need this drama, too.

Flynn wrote in the *Industrial Worker* newsletter published on December 15, 1909:

> *It certainly is a shame and disgrace to this city that a woman can be arrested because of union difficulties, bonds placed so high that immediate release is impossible, thrown into a county jail, where sights and sounds,*

On Stevens Street, many workers would climb on a box to shout out proclamations of abuse and their rights being stripped away. The Hotel Vendone and White's Hotel are in the background. *SPL/NWR.*

> *horrible, immoral and absolutely different from her ordinary, decent mode of life can be forced upon her. Her privacy invaded while trying to steal some sleep by a brute of a man in jail that hasn't attained the ordinary standard of civilization that requires a matron for the care of women prisoners. This all for law and order. O Liberty, what crimes are committed in thy name!*

To make matters worse for the department, Flynn was demanding a thorough investigation from a grand jury into the treatment of the male prisoners who were being denied medical attention because the hospital section of the county jail was being utilized for sexual intercourse with the female prisoners! But her demands were mostly ignored, and she seemed to get nowhere with the judges.

Flynn wrote on November 2, 1909:

> *We have appealed to the superior judges to give us the opportunity of getting at the matters through a grand jury, and here again we have met with refusal. We have no confidence in the honesty of purpose of the county prosecuting attorney in prosecuting criminal charges against city and county officials, as his action in the [Rose] Elliott case will show, inasmuch as he has not even yet brought a charge of betrayal and abortion against Officer Gilder, though he has confessions of the victim herself in the matter.*

Chief of Police Sullivan tried to improve the situation. He ordered three full-time matrons to work eight-hour shifts so that the female prisoners would now have a female attendant at all times, day and night.

The United States Constitution states that "Congress shall make no law abridging freedom of speech or of the press."

The *Spokane Chronicle* printed on December 14:

> *Is the city of Spokane clothed with authority to do that which the highest law-making body of this nation is expressly forbidden to do? Shall the city council of Spokane prescribe certain limits where the exercise of the Constitution's right of free speech shall be a crime, punishable by arrest, fine, imprisonment and insufficient food? Men and women are accused (and convicted) of criminal conspiracy for testing the validity of an ordinance that is unconstitutional and unlawful.*

The leaders of the IWW were recruiting other members from out of state to come help with the cause. Soon, hundreds of IWW men came to Spokane and began getting arrested for disorderly conduct and speaking on the streets. One after another, they were handcuffed and dragged to the jail.

The overflow of male prisoners were cramped into groups of twelve to twenty-six and shoved into cells that were only six feet by eight feet in size.

A large group of unidentified IWW men gathered together to protest for their rights. *LOC.*

When the jail could hold no more men, eighty-six men were hauled to the condemned Franklin schoolhouse that was used as a makeshift jail.

The treatment of the men was horrendous. Jaws were said to be broken, teeth knocked out; some were blinded. They were put in a sweat box (a room heated to extreme temperatures) for thirty-six hours at a time. For food, they were given only a few scraps of bread (sometimes moldy) and dirty water. In November, the IWW men went on a hunger strike. This would be another first for Spokane: it would be noted as the city where the first hunger strike was conducted in the United States.

Seattle and Portland were threatening to send seven thousand of their IWW men to Spokane for the crusade of free speech. "We will not back down!" they warned officials.

When the IWW was gathering in a private meeting hall, it was raided by the police, and five prominent IWW leaders were arrested on criminal conspiracy charges. Mrs. C.M. Conners, wife of a fellow IWW worker, was run over by a wagon at Main and Stevens Streets in Spokane. She suffered a broken arm, and part of her arm was torn away. The driver did not even stop.

The problems and the hunger strike continued to escalate. Men were getting sick; some were dying. Officials were worried they were going to have to use stomach pumps to force food into the prisoners' mouths. Soon, $50,000 in lawsuits were filed against the City of Spokane.

By late December, the city had had enough, and the prisoners were freed from jail.

After the ordeal was over, one prisoner told of his experience, and his story was printed in the December issue of the *Industrial Worker*:

> *Our first night in the school was terrible. Police threatened to freeze, beat and torture to death if men did not go to work on the rock pile. Some leaders were in the sweatbox for thirteen days. Doctors finally ordered them released, fearing death from torture. We were told that it did not make much difference if we did die, as it only cost forty-nine cents to cremate us.*
>
> *We were always forewarned when an investigative committee would visit us, by extra precautions to rid the dark dungeons of filth and scatter the men around in cells so as to make them look less crowded. The sweat box would be emptied. Committee would always be rushed through and not allowed to consult prisoners, for fear of exposing the hellish conditions. When we finally broke our hunger strike after seven and a half days of fasting, we got eight ounces of stale bread morning and evening. This allowance was cut down from time to time till we got only three-fifth ounces morning and*

evening. Refusing to work on the rock pile at Fort Wright, we were locked in cells at night and had to urinate through the bars of cells, not even a bucket furnished. The bread caused constipation and men were known to go two weeks without passage. Just think, Elizabeth Gurley Flynn and Mrs. Frenett getting ninety and one hundred days in these death traps—and for what crime?

On March 4, 1910, the City of Spokane revoked the ordinance banning street speaking.

CHAPTER 3
PROHIBITION AND BOOTLEGGING

A s early as 1908, the *Spokane Press* began running articles about the need for Prohibition and the reduction of alcohol consumption by its citizens. It printed on July 15, 1908, "The Prohibition Party is the very friend and well-wisher of every enemy of the drunk curse!"

The State of Washington was eager to jump on the bandwagon and limit alcohol intake. In 1908, the Prohibition National Headquarters announced that, so far, there were eight states complying with the laws and 250 cities were on board.

Judge Turner told reporters, "We favor the submission to the voters of Washington a constitutional amendment prohibiting the manufacture or sale of spirituous liquors within our borders!"

Soon, a saloonkeepers' campaign was organized in retaliation.

They called themselves the Knights of the Royal Arch, and they were a group of liquor men, cigar dealers and their allies. Their goal was to combat Prohibition and keep their businesses thriving. One of their leaders, William Bachrach, seemed logical enough when he told the people, "Remove the objectionable features from a saloon and prohibition dies a natural death. Not a drop to a man who cannot control himself! Let us put ourselves right as businessmen before our fellow men. Let us cut off the minors, the drunkards, the tramps, the criminals, the dance halls and the vicious of every class and kind! The whole country should not be made to suffer for the weakness of a few!"

One example given was that of a Spokane man who was in jail a few years earlier because he beat his wife when he was drunk. When the judge asked him why he did it, the man said, "Well, Judge, when the whiskey is in, sense is out. When I went home Saturday night to my wife, she wanted money for necessities, and I had none to give. I was crazed with drink. I struck the woman who has stood by me through all of the hardships of life."

In 1919, the Eighteenth Amendment of the Constitution was changed to "prohibit the manufacturing and sale of intoxicating liquors." Then, in October the same year, Congress passed the Volstead Act, which allowed the law to actually be enforced, so the demand for Prohibition agents was at an all-time high. Prohibition finally came to a well-received end in 1933.

THE BUSINESS OF BOOTLEGGING was frowned upon and taken very seriously. During this time, the production and selling of alcohol was a felony, and distillers and traffickers could be shot and killed on the spot. Fortunately, most officers and officials drank too, so they were somewhat merciful.

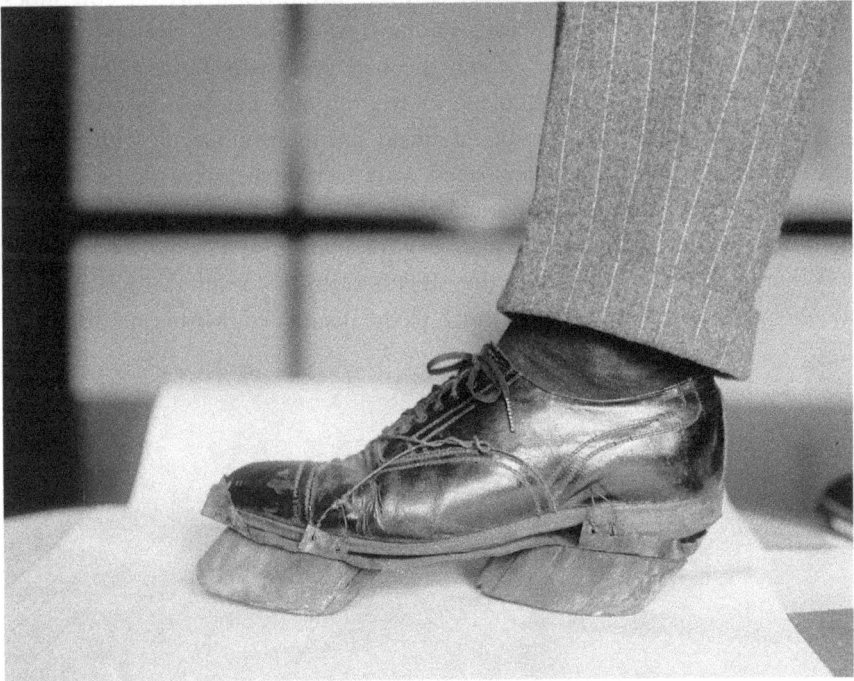

Bootleggers carved fake cow hooves out of wood and attached them to their shoes, so the police would not be able to track them as they checked their whiskey stills. *LOC.*

STOP GIRLS GOING INTO THE SALOONS

Mayor Daggett has sent to Chief of Police Waller orders to arrest all saloon men who allow girls who are not notorious characters in their places. The mayor thinks that saloon boxes are the ruin of girls and that the present plan is a good one and will work.

He also issued instructions to the detective department to allow no street walking in Spokane.

To try to control the chaos, Spokane mayor Daggett ordered Chief of Police Waller to arrest women of "notorious character" and also prohibited streetwalking. *The* Spokane Press, *January 25, 1906.*

Handmade whiskey stills were cropping up in hidden spots all over town. They were hidden in barns, in the woods, in basements, attics—anywhere they could be set up. The men who took to manufacturing alcohol illegally were termed "moonshiners." And they became experts at being discreet. The policemen had to search for stills on foot, since they were most often tucked away from obvious places.

The moonshiners were a crafty bunch, though. They developed a cunning way to trick the cops, to avoid being captured or followed. They carved fake cow hooves out of wood and attached them to their shoes! This way, the police would not be able to track them, as their tracks looked just like any other cow hoofprint. Some say the cow shoes idea sprang from a Sherlock Holmes story, in which the bad guy made horseshoes for his steed that looked like cow's hooves, not traditional horseshoes.

Men were not the only ones being sneaky during Prohibition. Women, too, got in on the action. They developed ways to hide a flask without obvious detection. Tiny flasks could be snuck into a boot or a cane. They could even be hidden discreetly beneath a woman's lacy garter.

When a raid was successful, the officers promptly poured the barrels of alcohol down the sewer drains, much to the dismay of thirsty onlookers.

CHAPTER 4

SPOKANE'S HOUSES OF ILL REPUTE

E arly Spokane was not an innocent city, and the citizens had their fair share of illicit interests. Although the city officials tried to outlaw drinking, gambling and whoring, they did not get very far. Even if they made laws to prohibit these things, it was very difficult to enforce them. Houses of ill fame were nestled in between banks, stores, shoe shops and even across from city hall! Their businesses were considered a necessary evil by Spokane citizens and officials. The cribs seemed to be everywhere, beckoning to lonely and horny men. Spokane's Skid Row cropped up near Howard Avenue and Front Street and ran for several blocks, butting up against Riverside and Sprague. A city ordinance was in place that would fine people one hundred dollars for prostitution and vagrancy, and sometimes even jail time was enforced. But the girls simply showed up on the first of every month to plead guilty and offer their five dollars. This became a good, dependable source of monthly revenue for the city. In 1888, Sandborn Insurance maps show two of these bawdy houses listed at 16 East Front Avenue and 112 Stevens Street.

Some of Spokane's more notorious ladies of the night were Dirty Dora, Bronco Liz, Irish Kate, Big Bertha, Leah Spaulding, Myrtle Gray and Flo Darling.

Big Bertha ran a theater in 1910 that was located on the corner of Bernard and Main Streets. Before that, she ran her business (competing with Frank Bruno's) on the Yale Block in town. Not much more is known about Big Bertha.

A little more is known about Dirty Dora. She ran away from her hometown of Missoula, Montana, in 1901. She lived at the Davenport Hotel in Spokane for a while. In 1903, she hooked up with a bad character named "Smokey" John Lennon, who was a barber but hated to work. Smokey was always in trouble with the law. He was a freeloading, good-for-nothing kind of guy. He threatened Dora with her life if she didn't pay the twenty-five cents to rent a room for the two of them. On October 30, Smokey was arrested for living in sin with Dirty Dora at a lodging house on Sprague Avenue. He said they had a marriage license, but he could not produce it. Then his story changed, and he claimed he only escorted Dora to balls and parties, nothing more. Lennon's real name was Grinnell. He got in more trouble when their landlord, Mrs. E. Mead, supplied information to officials, stating, "Mr. Grinnell introduced the woman to me as his wife and was heard to threaten her life unless she produced twenty-five cents for him!" There was a Dirty Dora who worked a stint for the circus for a while, eating mud as her showpiece attraction, but it is unclear if this was the same Dirty Dora.

Flo Darling was the most politically daring of the group of bawdy women. In 1902, she ran her house of ill repute on Front Street. In 1904, she became entangled in a long and difficult legal battle against an enraged citizen named E.E. Dempsie. Dempsie owned land in town, and he felt her whorehouses were devaluing his property. He filed suit against Flo for damages. He wanted to purge Front Street of all boardinghouses that were sheltering these "soiled doves." The woman offered to legitimately buy his property. He promptly put a ridiculous price—$9,000—on his land opposite city hall and demanded Flo purchase the twenty-two feet of the street-front parcel from him for this exorbitant price. But Flo was no dummy. She knew his piece of land was overinflated in price and refused to fall for his antics. She argued that the bank next door just secured forty feet of storefront property for only $7,000, so why was he asking so much for his parcel?

Frustrated, Dempsie wanted to fight. He knew his land was only worth about $4,500, but he wouldn't give in. He demanded arrests be made. His pursuit to rid Spokane of houses of ill fame came to be known as "Dempsie's Ban."

In October, the police finally caved, and the city proclaimed that it was illegal for men to be landlords of women who were running houses for immoral purposes. The chief of police, Waller, wrote up warrants for three men in particular who owned buildings with whorehouses in them: L.B. Whitten (who owned the Del Monte, run by Leah Spaulding), Archie Ash (who owned the Castle, run by Myrtle Gray) and F.S. Barrett (who owned the Windsor, run by Flo Darling).

From the stand, Flo proudly admitted she ran the Windsor. She also disclosed her future plans to open a new boardinghouse. She had saved her money and purchased ten acres of land near Dishman's Mill, just outside of town. With a big smile, she told everyone, "I am going to open the sweetest resort for immoral men and women in the state!" She boasted it would have a well-stocked bar with a big dance hall, a café and a ballroom. She also said that E.E. Dempsie should not be allowed to buy any land in that neighborhood in order to cause her more trouble. She was planning to hold an extravagant grand opening in the spring of 1905.

Possibly because they enjoyed Flo's gusto—or possibly because the men were eager to visit her new place of business—the court agreed that Dempsie's suits were mostly for his own profit, and the judge decided that there was not a law in place that catered to Dempsie's real estate and financial needs. Flo was allowed to run her new business outside of town.

But Flo's plans were parlayed again in 1909, when Spokane decided it needed to go "dry." She was running a very busy house of ill repute on East Sprague Avenue at the time. The town was changing the township boundary lines, and her Windsor place was within the confines of the Opportunity township (east of the city limits). Flo tried to secure votes for her section to be designated "wet," so she could continue her business. Unfortunately, the township voted "dry," and her roadhouse went out of business.

Spokane's soiled dove Bronco Liz had troubles of her own.

The famous working girl's real name was Ione Jane Whitney Skeels, but she was nicknamed "Bronco Liz." As she did not ride horses, one can only speculate as to how she acquired her nickname. She supposedly competed with two other famous nearby ladies of the night, Molly b'Damn and Terrible Edith. Liz was known as the local dance hall queen and a popular entertainer.

Liz met her soon-to-be husband, Charles "Chas" W. Skeels (1860–1889), while he was working with the local mines and she was entertaining the lonely miners. Skeels had originally come from Huntingtonshire, England, and crossed the sea in 1871 to make his new life in New York City before heading west. At the time of their attraction, Mr. Skeels had a wife and two children at home, and his affair with Liz had to be kept secret. Skeels was so in love with Liz that he enticed her to marry him as soon as he was granted a divorce from his wife. He devised a wild plan to do this: he suggested Liz cut off all of her hair, dress in men's clothing and go to work on his family's ranch in Choteau, Montana, until he could finalize his divorce.

Liz agreed to the arrangement, and soon, she became a working hand instead of a working girl. She continued to work on the farm, with no one the wiser that she was actually a girl. After several months, Skeels did get his divorce, and the couple went to Moscow, Idaho, to get hitched on January 2, 1888.

Instead of the honeymoon Liz expected, Skeels sent her back to Montana to "wait" for him. She did so suspiciously, until February came around. The new bride had a feeling something was up.

Liz soon caught wind of a rumor that Skeels was sleeping with another woman, an actress named Frankie Howard who worked at the Theater Comique. They met often at her love nest in a building known as Actor's Flat at 412 Howard Street in Spokane.

Liz became furious and went to find her husband, but not before getting her hands on a pistol (she had shot him once before while they were in Cascade, Montana). Liz's choice of weapon was a .32-caliber British Bulldog revolver that she had found at a pawnshop. The pawnbroker emptied the cartridge, but Liz was so determined to teach her husband a lesson that she roamed the district until she finally found someone to load the gun for her.

Liz worked out a plan to trick her cheating husband into coming out of hiding. She called for a messenger boy, and she paid the boy to look for Skeels and give an urgent message to him that he was needed at home because she was not feeling well. The boy quickly ran around town, looking for the bamboozling husband, but Skeels was not in any of the saloons in town.

Furious, Liz took matters into her own hands.

Liz and the boy traveled over to the Flats to scare her husband.

After much knocking on the apartment's entry by the boy, a very frustrated Skeels finally opened up the door. Disgruntled and irritated at being interrupted, Skeels left the room and entered the hallway, where Liz was waiting for him. Knowing he was caught red-handed, Skeels instantly became afraid of Liz, as she had shot him once before during their relationship.

He put up his hands and said, "Don't you make any breaks at me—keep away! I'm through with you forever!"

Liz did not listen. She fired the pistol at him, and three bullets entered his body. One went through his left arm and lodged in his stomach. The second bullet hit his right side. The third one secured a spot in his lower back.

Skeels yelled, "Let up firing your gun, Liz, or you will kill me!"

Liz looked her husband straight in the eyes, and without any hesitation, she pulled the trigger.

The fourth bullet somehow went wayward—luckily for Skeels.

Without further ado, Liz promptly turned on her heels and calmly made her way out from the Flats and headed back home. Skeels, somehow unaware of the extent of the damage she had done to him, slowly followed her. But he didn't get far. Bleeding profusely, he had to stop at a nearby store's doorstep. A man named D.S. Cowgill heard Skeels moaning as he cried out, "Some of you gentlemen, help me!"

As the blood slowly drained from Skeels's body, a carriage was called. After ten or fifteen minutes, the carriage arrived and took him to his saloon. The men carried him upstairs, where he wanted to lie down. A very rough-looking woman answered the door, possibly a working girl from the Pantheon. Soon, Drs. Essig and Parmlee attended to Skeels's wounds, but they both thought the shots were fatal and that he would surely soon be dead.

Officer Gillespie made his way to Liz, promptly told her she was under arrest and kept her confined to her residence until Sheriff Glispin and Officer McKernam could take her off to jail.

The *Spokane Falls Review* noted that she told them, "Of course I won't deny I shot him, but I was driven to it. I was crazy with jealousy! Since I married him, he has never been true. I met him in the Coeur d'Alene mines....When I heard he was now living with a woman named Alice somebody...it made me wild!"

T.W. Murphy and Thomas Griffits were hired to defend poor Mrs. Skeels, also known as Bronco Liz.

The philandering Mr. Skeels died from his wounds the next day while resting at his son Alfred's home. He was surrounded by his mother, three brothers and his two children from a former wife.

The trial for Skeels's murder lasted nine days, and the jury deliberated for forty-eight hours. The jury found Liz not guilty, and she was acquitted. They felt the verdict was justified by the evidence that Skeels was a bad man and a danger to the community.

Even if Skeels was considered locally a bad man, almost five hundred people attended his funeral.

The *Lewiston Teller* reported on January 2, 1890, that one reporter said, "We don't believe Liz should have been hanged, but she should have been punished to some extent."

It is said that hell has no fury like a woman scorned—and that appears to be true.

The Sunday Law Invites Trouble

The Sunday Law prohibited the selling and drinking of alcohol from midnight Saturday through a specified time on Sunday. This was supposed to halt the bad habits of people drinking on Sunday instead of spending time with their family and/or going to church services. Although the idea seemed promising, it failed on many levels.

One such example is the senseless murder of a Finlander named Victor Likka at the Elm Bar at 246 Main Avenue in Spokane. Likka had gotten into a small fight with Oscar Lingquist (also known as Lindquist), a fight that three witnesses claimed Likka did not provoke.

On the evening of June 4, 1909, patrons of the Elm were enjoying sharing a few drinks with friends. The bar owners, Hilda Johnson and Herman Olsen, were violating the Sunday Law by serving spirits, but they did not care. They were open for business.

Lingquist was becoming pretty intoxicated and soon became irritated with Likka. The nearby Officer Long was roused and came into the Elm to see what the fuss was about. After a loud argument and a brief struggle, Lingquist produced a big knife and began swinging it at Likka. Soon, Likka was fatally stabbed and fell to the floor, gushing blood. Then he ran out of the Elm and into the street.

Officer Long witnessed the whole thing. He quickly followed Lingquist one and a half blocks, until Lingquist turned around and started poking his knife at the officer. Long overpowered Lingquist and soon had him in handcuffs.

Likka was rushed to the hospital but sadly died on the way there.

CHIEF OF POLICE SULLIVAN promptly ordered the Elm closed. Lingquist was arraigned for murder before Judge Mann for killing Likka. He was also denied bail. A. Mattson, Hilda Johnson and Herman Olsen were placed under bonds to appear as witnesses in Superior Court and were told they needed to disclose any and all details of the murder. Hilda told the police, "I saw Lingquist in the rear of the Elm Bar flourishing a long knife and threatening to kill all in the house on the afternoon before the murder."

Lingquist professed no knowledge nor memory of the killing.

The Elm Bar was known to be a place of trouble caused by over-pouring whiskey.

Oscar Lingquist
murdered Finlander
Victor Likka at
the Elm Bar at
246 Main Avenue.
WSA/CD.

- A man named William Lindsey, a Finlander, was arrested at the Elm and sent to jail for cutting a man named Jack Reback, also a Finlander, in a fight at the saloon. Lindsey stated that he got mad at Reback for not buying more drinks, so he decided to stab him.
- Tom Martin was declared temporarily insane due to booze consumption when he decided to break the front windows of the Elm Bar.
- An unknown Finlander was robbed and beaten senseless to the point of not remembering his name and tossed into the alley behind the Elm.
- A man named Matson was jailed for public intoxication, and when he was questioned, he told the officers that he was a live snake–eater named Boscoe. Officer Walker asked him, "What's yer name?" "B-o-s-c-o-e. Boscoe, the live snake–eater! Yes-zer!" He was held in a cell to sleep off the whiskey.

CHAPTER 5

THE COLLAPSING OF THE
MONROE STREET BRIDGES

Spokane built three bridges called Monroe: one built from wood, one from steel and finally one from concrete.

The original bridge was built in 1888. It was designed to accommodate horses, wagons and pedestrians. It cost the city $42,500 to construct, but tragically, it burned down on July 22, 1890.

The second bridge was made of steel around 1892, after much debate. It was 1,099 feet long and appeared strong and everlasting. Mrs. Mary Winitch was the very first person to walk across it. It cost the city $107,000 to build.

But it was soon discovered that the bridge vibrated heavily. By 1905, the bridge was deemed unsafe, and only the bravest of individuals would cross it.

This bridge became compromised, possibly because of a mudslide on the south side that had deteriorated its strength. When the Ringling Brothers Circus came to Spokane in 1907, the elephants refused to walk across the bridge; some later said the animals could sense it was not trustworthy.

After a few years of use, the bridge showed signs of collapsing. The city engineer had cables attached to the bridge, as it was threatening to fall to the east. Later, they added additional braces, as it was swaying toward the west. Prior to the collapse, W.T. Roy, the superintendent of bridges, claimed, "It has been out of plumb for over a year, ever since fill was put on Main Street. But I do not feel it is in any danger of collapse." Boy, was he wrong! At the south end, the bridge had shifted an entire foot in a single year. During its collapse, two workers, J.F. Wolpers and A.M. Nelson, were both terribly hurt

The first Monroe Street Bridge was built in 1888 to accommodate horses and pedestrians, but it burned down in 1890. *SPL/NWR.*

A side view of the second Monroe Street Bridge, with a cable car crossing it and the raging Spokane River below. *WSA.*

Top: The remains of the ruins of the first Monroe Street Bridge, with the second one and the C and C Milling Company in the background. *SPL/NWR.*

Bottom: The massive group of Ringling Brothers Circus elephants. When the circus came to Spokane in 1907, the elephants refused to walk across the second bridge. *LOC.*

and rushed to Sacred Heart Hospital. They later sued the city for $10,000 in damages. The city ended up scrapping the bridge and selling seventy-five tons of metal to the Seattle Steel Company for $7.50 per ton.

THE THIRD AND FINAL bridge caused even more ruckus and debate, due to the high expense and expectations. The huge project developed more

The beautiful third Monroe Street Bridge in 1913, with the American Theatre and Hotel behind on the left and the Washington Water Power Company on the right. *LOC.*

drama and scandal, as designer John Chester Ralston eventually had to be removed from the project. He was accused of stealing the design from the Rocky River Bridge Company in Cleveland, Ohio. Ralston was charged with bad faith and hoodwinking city council. The revised plan Ralston submitted was not the same one previously approved by Professor Burr of the city planning group. Perhaps Ralston, knowing he was caught, tried to slip in a different design?

Ralston was in more trouble with the iron workers' union, too. He was protested by them because he wanted to use day labor. John Gore, secretary for the union, said, "This talk of the day labor plan being for the interest of the workingmen is all bosh! Ralston is an enemy of the labor and will run every scab workman in the country if he has his way. He says he will build the bridge for $312,000, but if the city gets short of $400,000 to $500,000, it is lucky. It will be cheaper in the long run for the city to lose every dollar it has so far invested in the bridge than to have Ralston build it. Under the plan Ralston has adopted to remove the old bridge and build the new one, there will be loss of life and heavy damage suits against the city....If the city permits Ralston to go ahead with this job it will regret it as he is wholly incompetent to carry on the work."

Nevertheless, the project moved forward, and the bridge was constructed from five hundred tons of steel and concrete. It was designed by the two famous Spokane architects Kirtland Cutter and Karl Malmgren. It is still classified as a beautiful city landmark. In 1911, the bridge, with its 281-foot-long concrete center span, was the largest concrete bridge in the United States and third longest in the world.

But the project was not a simple one, and workers were held by cables over the swift, raging river, making the task even more perilous. The freezing waters below ran 140 feet deep and 1,500 feet wide and flowed at an incredible 40,000 cubic feet per second. First, they had to tear down the remains of the original bridge. Then an extremely violent windstorm in July brought more trouble and problems. During this troublesome phase, two workers were tragically killed: George Parr and Carl Bentson (or Benkson).

The project exceeded its original cost and finally reached $535,000, half of which reportedly went toward labor (but this could be disputed). Labor rates in 1911 were just $3.50 per man per day (later increased to $5.00 per

A celebration of the Chicago, Milwaukee & St. Paul Railway crossing over the second Monroe Street Bridge in 1914, with hundreds of Spokane's citizens. *WSA.*

day); common labor was $2.75 per day, later increased to $3.00 per day. The bridge demanded 240,000 labor hours. The bridge was officially opened during a ceremony on November 23, 1911, and over three thousand happy Spokane citizens showed up to celebrate.

ONE PARTICULAR ADDITION TO the bridge's construction was the ornate bison skulls added to the sides of the four pavilions. Eight beautiful skulls in total adorn the bridge. The reason for adding these creative bison skulls is unclear. Original drawings submitted show American Indians with canoes on the pavilions and bison skulls located under the arches. Cutter and Malmgren's drawing showed the bison skulls attached where they currently are. The symbolism of the skulls is also unclear, but Cutter remarked later that the skulls were "installed for personal reasons," possibly inspiration gathered from his visit to Montana. Others claim the bison represent and honor those who came to the West on the Oregon Trail.

In 1914, a dedication ceremony for the new railway trestle built over the Monroe Street Bridge was a success, and hundreds of people attended. But the trestle was later considered an eyesore and was removed in 1974.

The bridge was listed in the National Register of Historic Places in 1976. Today, it has been reconstructed and is a beautiful pride and joy for Spokane.

CHAPTER 6

THE GREAT SPOKANE FIRE OF 1889

The citizens of Spokane were resilient and determined; absolutely nothing could stop them from achieving their goals and dreams. This attitude was never more prevalent than when the Great Spokane Fire of 1889 completely destroyed thirty-two city blocks. Within a few hours, every building and business within those blocks was reduced to ashes. The fire cost millions and millions of dollars in damages. Unfortunately, most of the businesses were poorly insured or not insured at all, leaving many owners with empty pockets.

At 6:15 p.m. on August 4, 1889, flames began shooting out of the roof of a lodging house near the Northern Pacific train depot on Railroad Avenue. The original cause of the flames remains a mystery to this day, but there were three theories.

- A spark from a passing train on the tracks;
- A man named Bill Wolfe cooking pork chops at the café in the rear of the building;
- A prostitute named Irish Kate, who was fighting with a patron when she decided she needed to go "fix her hair." She went upstairs to her room and heated her curling iron. The patron followed her upstairs and the argument continued, until someone knocked over a kerosene lamp, which started the fire.

After the devastating fire of 1883, Spokane citizens calmly deal with the aftermath and destruction. The beautiful Glover house is marked with an *X*. *SPL/NWR.*

A very smoky Riverside Avenue in 1889, after another Spokane fire destroyed the city. *SPL/NWR.*

Four brave No. 1 Station Spokane firemen pose in 1890, while a small boy sits on the sidewalk to the right. *WSA.*

THE *SPOKANE FALLS REVIEW* described the scene in its August 6, 1889 edition:

> *The terrifying shrieks of a dozen locomotives commingled with the roar of the flames, the bursting of cartridges, the booming of giant powder, the hoarse shouts of men, and the piteous shrieks of women and children. Looking upward a broad and mighty river of flame seemed lined against the jet-black sky. Occasionally the two opposing currents of wind would meet, creating a roaring whirlwind of fire that seemed to penetrate the clouds as a ponderous screw, while lesser whirlwinds danced around its base, performing all sorts of fantastic gyrations....In this manner the appalling monster held high carnival until about ten o'clock, when with a mighty crash the Howard Street Bridge over the Spokane River went down.*

The account of the blaze was quite horrific, and the heat and smoke were devastating. From the lodging house, the fire hopped across the street and torched the Ross house and the Pacific Hotel. Inside the engulfed Pacific Hotel, a poor unnamed woman was trapped. As she screamed for help, no one could offer her any. Crazed, she leapt from the widow on the second

A Model T touring car adapted to be used for fires, equipped with hoses and gear, with an unknown man and woman. *WSA.*

Two unidentified men test the water truck for the Spokane Fire Department. *WSA.*

The southeast corner of Riverside Avenue and Stevens Street, showing the second full block of Riverside. The Tull Building (five stories) is on the right. The post office (three stories) was attached to the Granite Building on the left around 1899. *Bertrand Studio, Teakle Collection, SPL/NWR.*

story and was killed immediately. Within minutes, the entire hotel crumbled to the ground, and all that was left was the chimney.

A strong wind picked up, creating more havoc and increasing the flames. From the Pacific Hotel, the fire spread down First Street to the next block, Hyde Block. Here it burned the entire section between Mill and Howard Streets on Riverside Avenue. Next it crossed Howard and Stevens Streets and destroyed the Tull Block and the post office—where it finally started to die, due to the fact that it had already burned everything down.

Back over by where the fire started, it leaped across Sprague Street, destroying the Opera House and the Brown's Bank building. Next it razed the Grand Hotel and the Frankfort Block (the largest building in Spokane at the time). The nearby Arlington Hotel was next to go up in flames.

At the grand Arlington Hotel, a man named Charles Davis was screaming for help out a third-floor window, but there was absolutely no way to get to the man to offer him assistance. As firefighters and locals stood by helpless, they watched the desperate man jump from the window down onto Howard Street below with a horrible thump. His clothes were on fire. Surprisingly, the man somehow managed to get up, and people swarmed to assist him.

But their efforts would be futile, for he had been burned so badly that most of his skin had peeled off, leaving a horrific sight. He was moved to safety but died shortly thereafter.

Desperate to slow the blaze, Mayor Firth ordered several buildings on Lincoln Street to be blown up with dynamite powder in the hopes of stopping the spread of the fire, but it was no use. The Cushing Building, the Washington Block and the Fall City Opera House were only a memory. With a loud crash, the Howard Street Bridge collapsed. The only buildings spared were the Crescent Building and the American Theater.

The courageous volunteer firefighters were desperately trying to stop the flames, but they had no water pressure in their hoses. The city's system was capable of pumping nine million gallons daily, but on this day, it was useless. By nine o'clock, thirty-two city blocks had been reduced to ashes, the once-grand structures now rubble. The Northern Pacific Railroad was the biggest loser: their new warehouse and all its contents—valued at over $1 million—completely gone.

At midnight, martial law was put into effect, because people were stealing whatever they could. To counter the robbing, people had to show a "pass" issued to enter the burnt area of town.

In 1889, many insurance adjusters set up desks in a makeshift office after the destruction of the Big Fire. *SPL/NWR.*

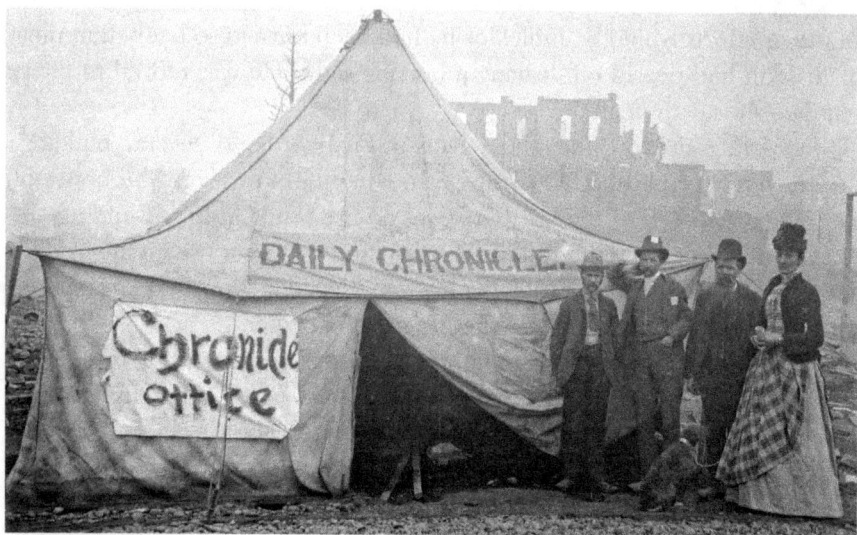

The *Spokane Daily Chronicle* newspaper office set up in a temporary tent in 1889 after the Big Fire. Three unidentified men, a woman and a dog pose. *The* Spokane Review.

Riverside Avenue and Post Street sometime after 1890. Many buildings were rebuilt bigger and better than ever after the Big Fire. *SPL/NWR.*

In the course of only three hours, most of Spokane's business district was no longer, two victims were dead and countless others were suffering from smoke damage to their lungs. The reports of damages ranged from 14 million to 30 million, and insurance adjusters were quick to set up makeshift offices in tents to help with what they could.

The next morning, as smoke from the smoldering remains of what was once their grand city lingered in the air, the citizens banded together and immediately made plans for how to rebuild Spokane—using mostly bricks and granite, of course. Businesses put up tents to continue their efforts. The *Spokesman-Review* printed later that month: "Perhaps in a year the devastated blocks will be rebuilt, and no traces will remain of the Great Fire. Spokane Falls is a necessity to eastern Washington."

And it was an accurate premonition, because Spokane *did* rebuild within the year and became even more grand, more spectacular, more safe and more dynamic than ever. No one was ever charged, and the original source of the fire was never officially determined.

BUT SOON AFTER THE fire, a dark cloud of shame disturbed Spokane's comradery. Two members of the common council and a police officer were caught misappropriating funds and supplies that were supposed to be used for the relief of the victims of the Great Fire. Sidney Waters, Peter Dueber and William Gillespie were soon charged, and warrants were issued for their arrests. Robert Inglis was also wanted, as it was reported that he was selling the stolen goods.

The men were stealing food items that were given freely to help those in need after the fire. In some cases, there was also forgery involved, and the money was being pocketed. Warrants for the criminals' arrests were signed by A.M. Cannon, the "Father" of Spokane. Waters and Dueber were requested to resign from city council, and Gillespie was court-martialed for conduct unbecoming of an officer. Inglis fled the minute he got word he was in trouble. But he soon returned to clear his name and take others down with him. Some men hurried to pay their debts to the committee, so it would not look like they had stolen, too. Major Walters ordered a load of provisions to be delivered to his house, instead of the headquarters. When Inglis heard of this, he confronted Walters, who told him, "Well, Inglis, everybody is getting in on this and I propose to make what I can of it, and you are a damn fool if you don't do the same!"

The boodlers (a person who profits from public subsidies) were accused that "they did then and there feloniously steal, take and carry away against the peace and dignity of the Territory of Washington." Mr. Gillespie had a $1,000 bond over his head that the prestigious E.B. Hyde and Colonel W.M. Ridpath of Spokane took care of. Inglis had to be tracked down from all over the place to be hauled back to Spokane; respectable chief of police Joe Warren traveled over five thousand miles to find him.

When all was said and done, it was noted that the boodlers stole ten hams equaling $25.00, two hundred pounds of syrup at $0.10 per pound, fifty pounds of bacon at $0.13 per pound, ten cases of canned goods at $3.00 per case, fifty pounds of coffee at $0.25 per pound and twenty-five pounds of tea valued at $0.80 per pound, for a total of $112.50.

CHAPTER 7

SPOKANE FALLS DYNAMITE EXPLOSION

One odd location in Spokane is an intersection at Division and Sprague that has earned the nickname "Death Corner." It is where a group of Spokane streets are divided all four ways—north, south, east and west—and it is an unlucky area to be avoided at all costs.

The gruesome story behind the area begins on September 6, 1890, when two hundred pounds of dynamite exploded during a Northern Pacific Railroad freight yard project. The job included the dangerous duty of removing a twenty-foot-high rock cliff and ledge—and thirty unlucky men were working directly underneath it when the terrible explosion occurred. In what was considered one of Spokane's deadliest tragedies, these thirty men lost their lives in a single instant, along with dozens of horses that were being worked to pull out the debris. Due to the extreme damage caused by over twenty-five thousand cubic feet of falling rocks crashing down in a flash, only fifteen of the thirty bodies could actually be recovered. The weight of the falling rocks made some of the bodies and a few horses nothing more than a memory.

Countless other workers were badly injured. Sadly, the actual names of many men were never revealed, as many immigrant men were "nameless"; they were often identified by only a number on a metal tag while on the job. During these times, men could drift and find odd jobs, signing in and out with an X or an assigned number. Some could not speak English or were evading the police but were willing to put in hard labor, so they were hired.

On this particular horrific and tragic evening, the dynamite was routinely placed and scheduled to detonate at exactly six o'clock, after most of the crew would have left for the day. But when the dynamite accidentally discharged twenty minutes early, the earth-shattering explosion caught all of the men off guard. Instead of heading home for the evening to spend time with their loved ones, they would never see their families again.

Foreman James McPherson and powder man Joseph Rhea were tamping the dynamite when it went off unexpectedly, killing both men instantly. During the long and careful three hours of laborious and sickening rescue efforts by brave men, nerves were rattling, as other charges were still in place and could go off at any minute, killing more men.

Many of the men who died were hardworking poor immigrants from all over the world. They were housed in a lower-end section of Spokane termed "Shantytown." Their bodies were buried in a mass grave plot at Greenwood Memorial Terrace. In honor of the men who lost their lives, a monument was placed near the graves by the Fairmount Memorial Association in 1996. A list of twenty-four known names has been compiled here: Henry Aptill, Louis Arlett, James Ballane, Henry Cobini, John Courtland, Nicola Dimottes, R. Erickson, August Fluron, Hugh Hayes, Jacob Hemine, F.A. Holm, Isaac Johnson, Gust Julien, Thomas Maher, William Maunsel, James McPherson, Home Oleson, Ray Pinkney, Andrew Puelonelio, Peter Raffalle, Joseph Rhea, James Tablo, Raffel Vetter and August Warm. The name John Castner also comes up as one of the victims.

CHAPTER 8

THE INFLUENZA EPIDEMIC OF 1918

I   t was panic.

During 1918, the newspaper headlines brought more than the daily news—they brought fear and panic about the flu that was killing so many people. When people developed the symptoms of the Spanish flu, their time on this planet was numbered, as most died within a few hours. The flu hit Washington the hardest during the first week of October in 1918. By the time it had raged through the state, almost five thousand people had died from it.

During its height, the Spanish flu affected over 500 million people (one-third of the world's population) and took over 50 million lives in the year it went viral. Over 675,000 were dead just in the United States alone. People were completely panicking, fearing for their lives. The virus had a short run, as it only lasted a little over a year, but it came in three deadly waves.

The mayhem started in March of 1918, and the flu-like symptoms were first reported in Kansas. Since World War I was happening, hundreds of thousands of soldiers were being shipped across the country and over the Atlantic Ocean during May.

In September, Boston, Massachusetts, got hit hard, primarily at Camp Devens United States Army camp. Of the 14,000 men stationed at Devens, 757 died from the Spanish flu.

October in Philadelphia was a nightmare. Corpses were piled up in any available cold storage. At one time, there were five hundred bodies waiting

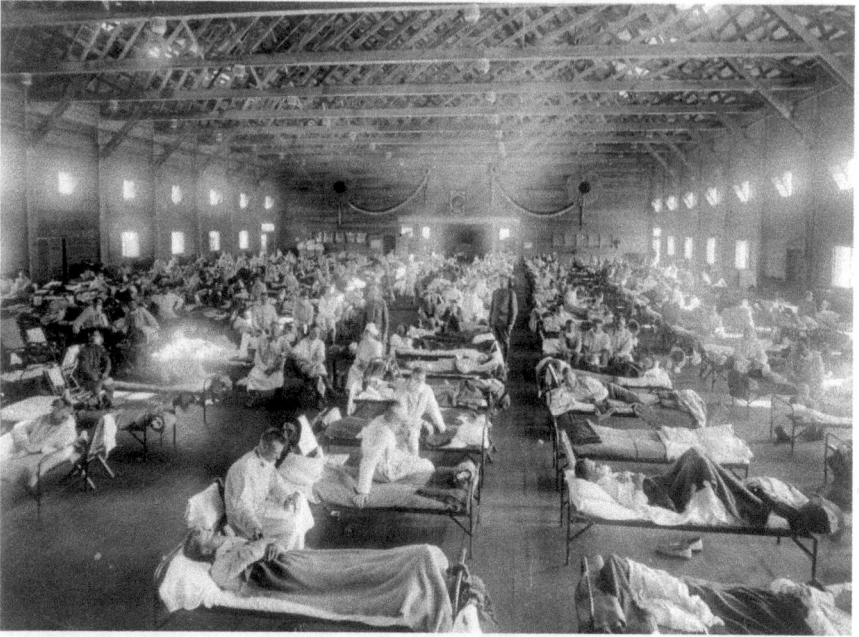

Dozens of suffering patients lying in emergency makeshift hospital beds during the influenza outbreak at Camp Funston, an army training camp in Kansas, 1918. *Otis Historical Archives, National Museum of Health and Medicine.*

Several police officers during the influenza panic in 1918, wearing masks made by the Red Cross. *WSA.*

to be buried! The New Year brought a third wave of pandemic paranoia and panic, for this was the deadliest strain of it yet.

Back in Washington, the Board of Health reported to Governor Ernest Lister:

> *This pandemic made its appearance in Washington in the first week of October. In the history of the State Board of Health no such calamity has afflicted the State nor has so serious an emergency ever arisen. In the five years 1913–1917 inclusive, from the five most common contagious diseases…there have been 1,768 deaths. From influenza alone we have had to date well over 2,000 deaths and the end is not yet. The toll will probably be double or triple 1,768. City health officers, except in Seattle, Tacoma, Spokane and Yakima, are part-time men. Their salary is often nothing or five dollars a month. They are appointed by their mayors and change frequently. They are not of our making and do not feel as if they have much responsibility to us. Their jobs pay little, and their policy is to do as much as the pay justifies.*

Dr. Thomas D. Tuttle, the state's health commissioner, stated:

> *The epidemic struck our state in the early part of October. The immediate introduction of the disease was through a shipment from Pennsylvania to the United States Naval Training Station at Bremerton of about 1,500 men, a large percentage of whom were afflicted with influenza when they reached their destination. From this location the disease spread widely [but] many outbreaks were not directly traceable to the infection at or near Seattle.*

The city determined that starting October 8, all places in Spokane that warranted large gatherings would be closed: theaters, schools, saloons, poolrooms, stores and churches. Funerals and weddings were banned.

Luckily, by summer, the influenza died down and eventually went away.

WASHINGTON HAD SUFFERED THROUGH pandemics before 1918.

In 1909, official health officers and Spokane's health department agents urged people to clean up the streets. The common housefly was considered the super-spreader for diphtheria and other diseases. They claimed Spokane's garbage system was to blame, along with the horse manure piled up in the streets.

In 1907, it was scarlet fever that raged through the city. Scarlet fever forced over forty thousand citizens to be quarantined within a twenty-mile radius of Spokane.

The year before that, in 1906, the fear was over typhoid fever, with which sixty-four people were infected in Spokane. Officials discovered it was largely due to people dumping their sewage into Spokane's drinking water system. Health officials felt that 75 percent of all the typhoid cases could have been prevented.

In the midst of our own pandemic, it is both frightening and oddly reassuring that this is not the first time America has faced a flu plague—and it probably won't be the last.

BIBLIOGRAPHY

An excellent general source for early Spokane history is the *Spokane Falls Review* New Year's Edition, December 29, 1887.

Spokane's Ruthless Italian Gang: The Black Hand

Spokane Press, December 10, 1906; July 2, September 2, 8, 14, 1907; November 7, 10, December 12, 1908; August 3, 1909; April 8, September 23, 1910.

Dynamite Brings Up Bodies

Spokane Press, March 24–27, May 25–27, 1909.

Body Shot and Burned at Fort George Wright

Santa Fe New Mexican, January 12, 1910.
Spokane Press, March 24, May 27, 28, 1909.
Vancouver Daily World, April 6, 1909.

Killed over Bad Handwriting

Bamonte, Suzanne, and Tony Bamonte. *Life behind the Badge: The Spokane Police Department's Founding Years, 1881–1903.* Spokane, WA: Tornado Creek Publications, 2008.
Spokane Review, March 14, 1896.

Sheriff George Conniff: Killed over Milk and Butter

Arksey, Laura. "Newport City Marshall George Conniff Is Shot While Interrupting a Creamery Burglary on September 14, 1935." HistoryLink. April 21, 2009. https://www.historylink.org/File/8995.
Bamonte, Suzanne, and Tony Bamonte. *Life behind the Badge.*
Nome Daily Nugget, September 24, 1935.
Shelton, Keith. "Creamery Robbery Turns Deadly." Spokane Historical Society. https://spokanehistorical.org/items/show/202.
Unsolved Mysteries Wiki. www.unsolvedmysteries.fandom.com.

The Chinamen Murders

Spokane Press, July 3, 8, 9, 1907.

Jealous Husband Shoots His Business Partner

Spokane Press, October 11, 12, 1904.

Better Obey the Carons

Spokane Press, May 1, 1903; October 19, 1904; June 5, 1909.

A Frozen Baby and a Jealous Husband

Spokane Press, February 21, 1910.

Schultz: Killed over a Paycheck

Spokane Press, December 9, 1907; May 25–29, June 17, 1908.

Death over a Dollar

Coeur d'Alene Press, October 21, 1907.
Daily Capital Journal, January 22, 1908.
Spokane Press, October 22, November 5, 21, December 21, 1907; January 22, 25, June 17, 1908.

Killed for a Couple of Horses

Spokane Press, May 12, 1906; January 11, 12, 30, 1907; June 6, 8, 1909.

The Brutal Murder of George Danieluk

Spokane Press, November 18–23, 1908.

Insane Man Kills His Wife

Spokane Press, January 25, 26, 28, 29, 30, February 4, 5, 20, April 9, 12, August 27, November 3, 1909.

Fantastic Duel in the Street

Spokane Press, October 25, 26, 1905.

Killed over a Free Meal

Spokane Press, July 22, August 19, 1905; May 23, 1906; February 28, 1908.

BIBLIOGRAPHY

Spokane's Hatchet Killer

Crime Museum. "The Dillon Massacre—Hatchet." https://www.crimemuseum.
    org/crime-library/mass-murder/dillon-massacre-hatchet/.
Evening Star, January 22, March 20, 1944.
Nome Nugget, January 21, 1944.
True Crime Library. "Woodrow Wilson Clark." https://www.truecrimelibrary.
    com/crimearticle/woodrow-wilson-clark/.
Ypsilanti Press, January 26, March 8, 1944.

Son Slays Father over Twenty-Five Dollars for a New Suit

Coeur d'Alene Press, August 29, 1906.
Spokane Press, November 21, 23, 26, December 1, 6, 24, 26, 1906.

Walla Walla State Penitentiary

Dougherty, Phil. "Twelve-Year-Old Herbert Niccolls Jr. Shoots and Kills
    Asotin County Sheriff John Wormell on August 5, 1931." HistoryLink.
    February 4, 2006. https://historylink.org/file/7634.
Find a Grave. https://www.findagrave.com.
Gibson, Elizabeth. "Nine Die in Escape Attempt at Washington State
    Penitentiary in Walla Walla on February 12, 1934." HistoryLink. April
    26, 2006. https://historylink.org/File/7650.

McNeil Island Corrections Center

Ott, Tim. "Robert Stroud Biography." Biography.com. Last updated August
    20, 2020. www.biography.com/crime-figure/robert-stroud-birdman-of-
    alcatraz.
Washington State Department of Corrections. https://www.doc.wa.gov.

The Man Who Escaped Two Federal Prisons and One Government Jail

Las Vegas Optic, July 3, 1913.
Spokane Press, February 21, 1910.
Tacoma Times, July 17–20, 1912.
Topeka State Journal, June 30, 1913.

Police Corruption and a Dead Baby

Spokane Press, May 9, 10, September 15, 21, 28, 29, October 25, November 10, 14, 26, 1910.

The IWW and the Banning of Free Speech

Gurley Flynn, Elizabeth. "Story of My Arrest and Imprisonment." *Industrial Worker* 1, no. 39 (December 15, 1909). https://archive.org/details/v1n39-dec-15-1909-IW/.
Leavy, Ed. "Labor History: The Spokane Free Speech Fight." http://svft.ct.aft.org/files/labor_history_-_december_2015.pdf.
Rieder, Ross, and the HistoryLink staff. "IWW Formally Begins Spokane Free-Speech Fight on November 2, 1909." HistoryLink. June 22, 2005. https://historylink.org/File/7357.
Spokane Falls Review, December 3, 16, 1909; March 27, April 10, June 7, November 2, 6, 8, 11, 1910.
Spokane Press, January 18, 1909.

Spokane's Houses of Ill Repute

Spokane Falls Review, June 30, 1883.
Spokane Press, November 25, 1902; October 30, 1903; July 14, October 20, 1904; January 8, December 16, 1908; March 3, 1909.

The Sunday Law Invites Trouble

Spokane Press, March 22, 1904; August 12, 1907; April 12, 19, June 4, 5, 16, 28, September 15, 1909.

The Collapsing of the Monroe Street Bridges

City of Spokane Historic Preservation Office. "Historic Properties of Spokane: The Monroe Street Bridge." https://www.historicspokane.org.
Nash, Paige M. "Monroe Street Bridge." Spokane Historical. Accessed August 13, 2021. https://spokanehistorical.org/items/show/507.
Spokane Press, January 3, 1907; March 9, July 22, 1910.

The Great Spokane Fire of 1889

Arksey, Laura. "Great Spokane Fire (1889)." HistoryLink. March 20, 2006. https://historylink.org/File/7682.
Helena Independent, August 17, 1889.
Spokane Falls Review, New Year's Edition, December 29, 1887; August 29, September 19, 1899.
St. Paul Daily Globe, August 19, 1899.
Wheeling Daily Intelligencer, August 6, 1889.

The Influenza Epidemic of 1918

Caldbick, John. "Flu in Washington: The 1918 'Spanish Flu' Pandemic." HistoryLink. March 23, 2017. https://historylink.org/File/20300.

Websites

Ancestry. https://www.ancestry.com.
Find a Grave. https://www.findagrave.com.
Library of Congress. https://www.loc.gov.
National Archives. https://www.archives.gov.
Washington State Archives. https://www.sos.wa.gov/archives/.

ABOUT THE AUTHOR

Originally from upstate New York, Deborah Cuyle loves everything about small towns and their history. She has also written *Kidding Around Portland* (OR), *Images of Cannon Beach* (OR), *Haunted Snohomish* (WA), *Ghosts of Leavenworth and the Cascade Foothills* (WA), *Haunted Everett* (WA), *Ghosts of Coeur d'Alene and the Silver Valley* (ID), *Ghosts and Legends of Spokane* (WA), *Ghostly Tales of Snohomish* (WA), *The 1910 Wellington Disaster* (WA), *Wicked Coeur d'Alene* (ID) and *Murder & Mayhem in Coeur d'Alene and the Silver Valley* (ID). Also soon to be released: *Wicked Spokane* (WA). Her passions include local history, animals, museums, hiking and horseback riding. Deborah, her husband and her son are currently remodeling a historic, crumbling mansion in Milbank, South Dakota, built in 1883.

Visit us at
www.historypress.com